THE EMPOWERED INVESTOR

THE EMPOWERED INVESTOR

7 Principles for Strategic Wealth
Creation in a New Financial World

CUNO PUEMPIN

Professor Emeritus of Strategy, St. Gallen University, Switzerland

HEINRICH LIECHTENSTEIN

Professor, IESE Business School, University of Navarra, Spain

FARIBA HASHEMI

Swiss Federal Institute of Technology, Lausanne, Switzerland

and

BRIAN HASHEMI

Managing Partner, Salus Partners SA, Switzerland

palgrave
macmillan

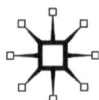

First published 2014 by
PALGRAVE MACMILLAN

Palgrave Macmillan in the UK is an imprint of Macmillan Publishers Limited,
registered in England, company number 785998, of Houndmills, Basingstoke,
Hampshire RG21 6XS.

Palgrave Macmillan in the US is a division of St Martin's Press LLC,
175 Fifth Avenue, New York, NY 10010.

Palgrave Macmillan is the global academic imprint of the above companies
and has companies and representatives throughout the world.

Palgrave® and Macmillan® are registered trademarks in the United States,
the United Kingdom, Europe and other countries

ISBN: 978–1–137–36686–3

This book is printed on paper suitable for recycling and made from fully
managed and sustained forest sources. Logging, pulping and manufacturing
processes are expected to conform to the environmental regulations of the
country of origin.

A catalogue record for this book is available from the British Library.

Library of Congress Cataloging-in-Publication Data

Puempin, Cuno, 1939–
    The empowered investor: 7 principles for strategic wealth creation in
a new financial worlds / Cuno Puempin, Professor Emeritus of Strategy,
St. Gallen University, Switzerland, Heinrich Liechtenstein, Professor,
IESE Business School, University of Navarra, Spain, Fariba Hashemi,
Swiss Federal Institute of Technology, Lausanne, Switzerland and
Brian Hashemi, Managing Partner, Salus Partners SA, Switzerland.
    pages cm
    ISBN 978–1–137–36686–3
    1. Investments. 2. Finance, Personal. I. Title.
    HG4521.P897 2014
    332.6—dc23   2014000951

CONTENTS

List of Figures   ix

List of Tables   xi

Introduction   xiii
  Who should read this book?   xiii
  Why should you read this book?   xiii
  Overview of the book   xiv
  About the authors   xvi
  Acknowledgments   xvii
  Disclaimer   xvii

**Part I   From Broken Investment Models to
Sustainable Strategic Investing**

1 Perils of the Misguided Investor: Lessons from
a CFO – Part 1   3

2 Why Traditional Investment Models Don't Work   5
  The truth about returns on stocks and bonds   5
  Taxes, fees, and other costs   9
  The temptation to follow simple graphs and the
    catastrophic effects of power laws   10
  So is investing a bell curve game?   12
  The tremendous impact of power law events   13
  Why is the financial services industry (still) promoting
    stocks and bonds?   15
  Challenges facing near-term performance   16
  Conclusion: what to expect from traditional
    investment concepts   17

3   The Investor Back at the Core of Investing: Lessons
    from a CFO – Part 2   19

4   The Essence of Strategy   25
        The battle of Salamis   25
        The core elements of strategy   27
        Strategic principles: universal laws of life   30

5   The Empowered Investor: A New Paradigm of Investing   33
        A framework for strategic wealth creation   33
        Strengths: the investor at the core of investment strategy   36
            The importance of strengths   36
            Why are strengths neglected in finance literature?   39
            How to build strengths   40
                Where can strengths be built?   41
                Concentrate!   43
                Assign resources   44
                Focus on allocation of resources   45
                Be aware of risks   45
        Opportunities: sources of wealth creation   46
            Opportunities in the finance industry   46
            Pitfalls of the finance industry   48
            Types of opportunities   48
            Finding opportunities: chance or methodology?   49
                Start with your strengths   50
                Do your homework: scan the environment   50
                Apply a long-term view   50
            Pitfalls of opportunities   51
        Networks: support of wealth creation   53
            Networks in finance   53
            Why are networks so important?   55
            Guidelines for building networks   56
                The heart of the network: core competences   56
                Networks are a two-way street   57
                Strong and weak ties   58
                Building your network strategy   59
        Differentiation: the path to uniqueness and competitive
            advantage   60
            Successful differentiation: William's story   60
            Prerequisites for successful differentiation   63
                Building core competences for differentiation   63

Apply an indirect approach   63
Be innovative   64
Threats and risks: preventing losses   65
Continuous wealth creation without setbacks is
    not possible   66
How to deal with threats and risks   67
    Rigorous analysis   67
    Careful selection of the core competences to be built 69
    Risk management by concentration of forces   69
    Avoiding threats and risks   70
    Use of options and derivatives   71
    Build networks   71
    Don't over-leverage   72
    Diversification   73
Timing: limited strategic choices   74
Guidelines for successful timing: cycles   74
    Apply the big picture   76
    Clarify your investment horizon   76
    Assure your strategic flexibility   77
    Be creative and courageous   77
    Be patient   78
Efficiency: a prerequisite for value creation   78
Fees can hamper wealth creation   78
    Using networks effectively   80
    Opportunity costs   80
    Be selective   83
Three dimensions of efficiency   83
Making use of the framework of strategic investing   84
Strategic asset allocation   85

Part II   How to Be a Successful Strategic Investor

6   Two Paths to Your Investment Strategy   91
    How Paul became a successful investor by crafting
        his strategy   91
    How Ralph designed his investment strategy with a
        formal process   93
    Crafting vs. designing strategy   94

7   What Should an Effective Investment Strategy Contain? 97
    The vision of the investor   97

The core competences the investor intends to build   99
The structure of the investment portfolio   99
    Examples   104
Handling threats and risks   107
The networks the investor intends to build and use   107
Guidelines for cash and liquidity   109
Priorities for allocation of investor resources   109
The legal and tax structure   110
    Example   110

8   Putting the Process of Strategic Investing into Practice   113
    Essential considerations   113
    Key questions to ask – information analysis   115
        Questions on strengths   115
        Questions on opportunities   116
        Questions on networks   117
        Questions on differentiation   118
        Questions on threats and risks   118
        Questions on timing   118
        Questions on efficiency   119
        Practical considerations   119
    Developing options as a step to success   120
        Creating alternative options   120
    The moment of truth – evaluating options and
        making decisions   122
    The hard work – implementing the strategy   123
    Ensuring success – strategic control   125

9   Putting Everything Together   127
    A final story: Henry's success   127
    Applying the framework to all aspects of wealth creation   131
    Final remarks on this new approach   131

Appendices   133

Notes   139

References   149

LIST OF FIGURES

I.1   Structure of the book   xv

2.1   Stock prices as measured by S&P 500, 1913–2013   6

2.2   Stock prices as measured by S&P 500, 2011–2012   6

2.3   Stock prices as measured by S&P 500, 2002–2012   7

2.4   Nominal vs. real returns   10

2.5   The Normal Distribution   11

4.1   The Battle of Salamis   27

4.2   Strategy framework, five forces   32

5.1   The framework of strategic wealth creation   36

5.2   Phoenix stock price   52

7.1   Martin's portfolio structure   100

7.2   Example of the overall structure of a portfolio for
      wealth creation   101

7.3   Portfolio structure of a 43-year-old investor   104

7.4   Portfolio structure of a 52-year-old investor   105

7.5   Portfolio structure of a 63-year-old real estate investor   106

8.1   The formal process of strategic investing   114

LIST OF TABLES

2.1	Bond real returns	8
2.2	Stock market events volatility	13
7.1	Description of the four portfolios of strategic wealth creation	103
7.2	Example of a simple investment strategy outline	111

INTRODUCTION

WHO SHOULD READ THIS BOOK?

This book is written for individuals and professionals whose objective is to build substantial wealth. Concentrating on the most important challenges facing an investor and using real world examples, we demonstrate how the Empowered Investor can develop and deploy an effective strategy to successfully grow his or her investments. Since the classical approach to strategy as practiced by the military, corporations, and other fields is not well known in financial literature, we embarked on this project to elucidate how the strategic principles of these disciplines can be applied to wealth creation.

WHY SHOULD YOU READ THIS BOOK?

If you have funds to invest as an individual or as a member of an organization, you probably want to know whether you can create substantial wealth from this starting amount. You may have already consulted financial organizations, such as banks and brokers, and read extensively in the academic, finance, and general literature, all of which heavily promote diversified investments in assets such as stocks and bonds (as well as products derived from these instruments). Our research suggests that this approach may help to preserve capital, but it is certainly not suitable for investors whose mission is to create substantial wealth. If financial instability, inflation, and higher taxes continue to mark the economic outlook, traditional approaches may fail to even preserve capital. Our experience illustrates that a paradigm shift is needed where developing an innovative strategic approach is essential for wealth preservation and wealth creation.

We start our discussion with the observation that investing always takes place in a dynamic social system where the rules of strategy must be applied. Therefore, we approach wealth creation from a strategic perspective to generate new insights and understandings. Over the last decade, the authors have had considerable practical experience making successful investment decisions, as well as occasional mistakes. This book draws from our experience as private investors and board members of financial institutions to provide an in-depth analysis of the strategic principles that make investors successful.

Several books by Cuno Puempin written during his tenure as professor of strategy at St. Gallen University, Switzerland, form the foundation for this book. Heinrich Liechtenstein's contribution is based on his position as professor of finance at Instituto de Estudios Superiores de la Empresa (IESE), in Barcelona, Spain. Fariba Hashemi's contribution is based on her experience as a faculty at various academic institutions including International Institute for Management Development (IMD) and Swiss Federal Institute of Technology (EPFL), in Lausanne, Switzerland. And Brian Hashemi contributed to this book through his decades of experience in application of strategy to investments, and through his role as Managing Partner of Salus Partners SA, in Lausanne, Switzerland.

OVERVIEW OF THE BOOK

This book is structured in two parts: Part I describes the basic facts about traditional investment concepts and introduces the essence of strategic investing. In Part II we discuss applying the framework to the process of developing and implementing an investment strategy.

Chapter 1 begins with a real case study of an investor whose initial negative experiences led him to reconsider and improve his investment approach. Chapter 2 discusses the shortcomings of traditional investment concepts, and Chapter 3 follows our investor from the first chapter to understand how he achieved outstanding results once he began applying a strategic approach.

Chapter 4 presents the main strategic elements developed in the military, corporations, and other fields. The core of the book is presented in Chapter 5, starting with findings from strategy and introducing a framework for developing, optimizing, and implementing an investment strategy.

Through our various interviews and practical experience we have identified different approaches for creating an investment strategy, and we describe the two most important ones in Chapter 6. Chapter 7

Figure I.1   Structure of the book

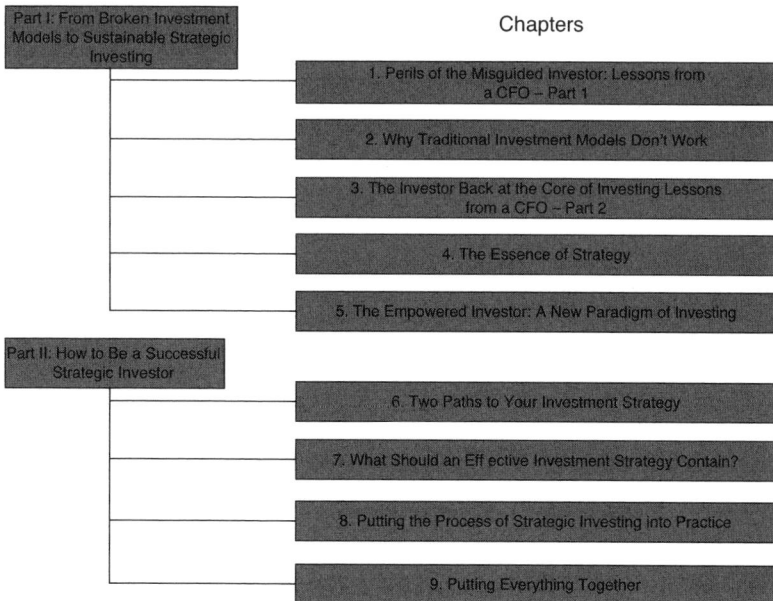

uses a practical example to explore the essential elements of investment strategy through a discussion of portfolio construction.

Chapter 8 focuses on the process of strategy development and its practical application, and Chapter 9 includes a final example of a highly successful investor where the different parts of strategic investing fit together.

ABOUT THE AUTHORS

Cuno Puempin is a Swiss entrepreneur, economist and private investor. He has served on many boards of directors and was a member of the international advisory board of the Blackstone Group in New York. In the past 20 years Dr. Puempin has successfully applied the seven principles of wealth creation presented in this book to his own private investments. He is a Professor Emeritus of Management and Strategy, and was Chairman of the Institute of Management at the St. Gallen University in Switzerland. Dr. Puempin is a regular speaker at leading global venues such as the World Economic Forum in Davos.

Heinrich Liechtenstein is the founder of a network of leading Angel investors in Germany, serves on the investment committee of a Family Office, and is advisory board member of a Private Equity firm. Dr. Liechtenstein is Professor of Finance in IESE Business School and specializes in entrepreneurial finance and management of wealth.

Fariba Hashemi is an economist with extensive experience in investment strategy and decision making. She has designed and instructed in Executive Education, Masters and Doctoral programs at International Institute for Management Development in Lausanne (IMD), The Graduate Institute in Geneva, Swiss Federal Institute of Technology in Lausanne (EPFL), and Karolinska Institute in Stockholm. Dr. Hashemi holds a PhD in Economics from the University of California in Los Angeles. She currently serves on the editorial boards of two academic journals in economics and finance, and is an advisor to a Family Office on wealth planning and management.

Brian Hashemi is a managing partner at Salus Partners S.A. in Switzerland, leading the healthcare investment practice of the firm. In this capacity he has successfully applied the strategic principles presented in this book for investments in proven medical innovations. Prior to establishing Salus Partners, Dr. Hashemi was a partner at a multi-family office leading the Direct Investment team. He holds a PhD in Applied Physics from Cornell University in New York, and an MBA in Entrepreneurship and Investment Management from The Wharton School in Philadelphia. Dr. Hashemi has been an Assistant Professor at Baylor College of Medicine where he began his affiliation in the National Space Biomedical Research Institute. For 13 years he was responsible for the development of advanced technologies in the biomedical division of NASA, a number of which were flown in the Space Shuttle program on STS-81 and STS-84.

ACKNOWLEDGMENTS

This book could only have been written with the support of many people, including our interview partners, colleagues in the academia, and successful strategic investors. We would also like to thank Samer Ajour for his research assistance, Nanci Healy for her editorial assistance, and Sonia Garcia for her ongoing back office work.

Our special thanks go to Theodore Margellos for his support.

DISCLAIMER

This book is for information purposes only and should not be construed as investment advice. Neither Palgrave Macmillan nor any of the authors make any representations or warranties regarding, or assumes any responsibility for the accuracy, reliability, completeness or applicability of, any information, calculations contained herein, or of any assumptions underlying any information, calculations, estimates or projections contained or reflected herein.

While this book represents the authors' understanding at the time it was prepared, no representation or warranty, either expressed or implied, is provided in relation to the accuracy, completeness or reliability of the information contained herein. The viewpoints presented in this book should not be regarded by the reader as a substitute for the exercise of his or her own judgment. Investing entails certain risks, including the possible loss of the entire amount invested. The reader should obtain advice from their own tax, financial, legal and accounting advisers to the extent that he or she deems necessary. No liability whatsoever is accepted for any loss (whether direct, indirect or consequential) that may arise from any use of the information contained in or derived from this book.

Part I

FROM BROKEN INVESTMENT MODELS TO SUSTAINABLE STRATEGIC INVESTING

Chapter 1

PERILS OF THE MISGUIDED INVESTOR: LESSONS FROM A CFO – PART 1

Martin Heller began his career as a certified public accountant in the late 1970s. A highly qualified young man, he spoke several languages and soon established himself as a successful professional in the financial services industry. He married, had three children, bought a roomy family home, and as his income grew he was able to pay off his mortgage and save a fair amount.

In 1990, with a small inheritance along with his savings, Martin began to search for a way to invest his money. Lacking investment expertise, he sought advice from other professionals including his banker and business club friends who were also active in finance. He recalled, "Everybody suggested that I put my money in stocks and bonds, either buying them directly or by investing in mutual funds." As a result he followed his banker's suggestion and invested in a portfolio of quoted stocks and bonds. By 1998, his net wealth had fallen by 25 percent, not only as a result of that year's crash but also due to high brokerage fees and taxes.

During our interview Martin concluded that "banks and their relationship managers have a significant conflict of interest with their clients. To maximize profits, the bank has to generate large brokerage fees and other revenues, which is in conflict with the interest of the client, who wants a portfolio that optimizes risk-adjusted returns with minimal transaction costs. The problem is that, even for a very client-oriented bank employee, the interests of the bank prevail because salaries and bonuses are tied to the revenues employees generate."

When his banker saw that Martin was disappointed with the investment approach, he attempted to propose other investments based on the so-called scientific models such as the Modern Portfolio Theory. But Martin felt unable to assess these options, and he soon became dissatisfied with the hefty fees he was paying: "I had the impression that my banker always wanted to keep the initiative on his side, that he wanted to prevent me from taking responsibility for my own investment decisions."

After discussions with friends who had similar experiences, Martin concluded that achieving satisfactory returns with his banker, perhaps with any banker, was highly unlikely. But he remained committed to building his personal wealth and achieving an annual return of at least 10 percent on his investments. He knew that he had to radically change his investment approach to achieve this goal.

Chapter 2

WHY TRADITIONAL INVESTMENT MODELS DON'T WORK

As long as Martin was investing according to his banker's recommendations he was not able to substantially grow his wealth. Bonds generated only low returns, and he still had to pay taxes on the returns. His stocks went up and down with the market without any reasonable logic. "I realized that with the conventional approach to investing in (quoted) stocks and bonds I would never be able to build real wealth," he confided in our interview. Why then does the financial industry heavily promote investments in these asset classes?

THE TRUTH ABOUT RETURNS ON STOCKS AND BONDS

When Martin's advisors were convincing him to invest in stocks, they used graphs of S&P 500 returns from 1980–2000 which showed an impressive average return of 15 percent. However, if we look over the last 100 years (see Figure 2.1), the annualized S&P 500 return is a fraction of that, at just 2.10 percent.

Figure 2.1   Stock prices as measured by S&P 500, 1913–2013

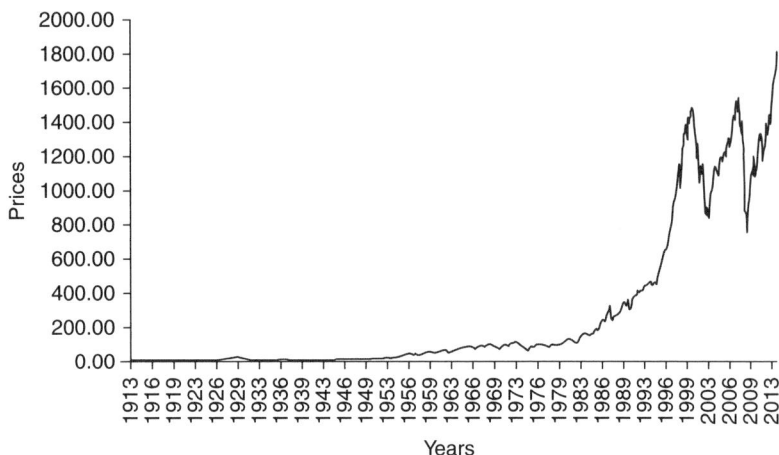

Source: S&P Capital IQ – capitaliq.com, S&P Historical Price.

True, with very good market timing – buying in September 2011 and selling in September 2012 – the annualized S&P 500 return would have been 24.83 percent.

Figure 2.2   Stock prices as measured by S&P 500, 2011–2012

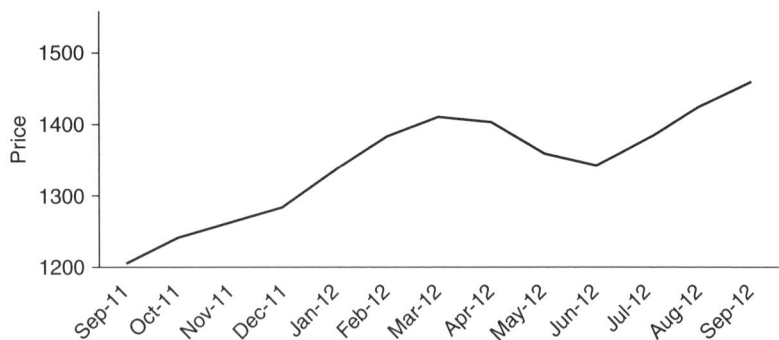

Source: S&P Capital IQ – capitaliq.com, S&P Historical Price.

But there is of course the other side of market timing: over the ten-year period from 2002 to 2012, an investor would have lost −0.35 percent.

Figure 2.3　Stock prices as measured by S&P 500, 2002–2012

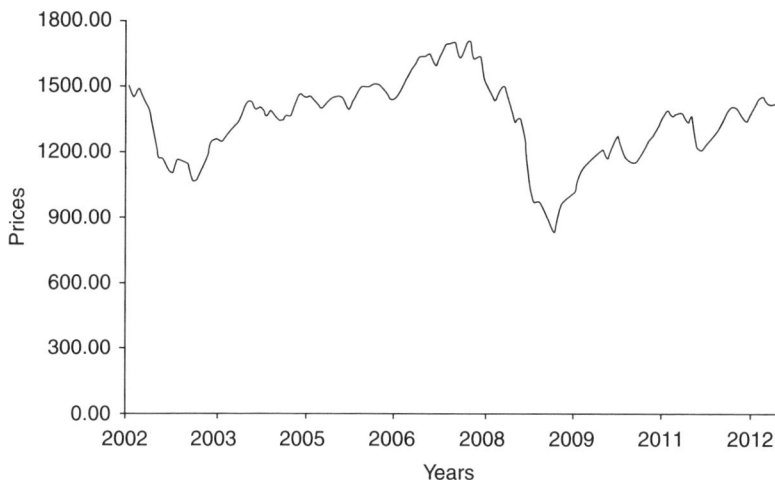

Source: S&P Capital IQ – capitaliq.com, S&P Historical Prices

Figure 2.3 illustrates that, to create wealth, an investor would have to apply a very difficult market timing. He would have had to invest massively in 2002, stay invested until 2007, sell all stocks in 2007, and again invest heavily in 2008 after the crash. Unfortunately, however, there is a fundamental difficulty in understanding market movements, even in retrospect. As the acclaimed economists George Akerlof and Robert Shiller[1] explain:

> The real value of the U.S. stock market rose over fivefold between 1920 and 1929. It then came all the way back down between 1929 and 1932. The real value of the stock market doubled between 1954 and 1973. Then the market came all the way back down. It then lost half of its real value between 1973 and 1974. The real value of the stock market rose almost eightfold between 1982 and 2000. Then it lost half of its value between 2000 and 2008. The question is not just how to forecast these events before they occur. The problem is deeper than that. No one can even explain why these events rationally ought to have happened even after they have happened. One

might think, from the self-assurance that economists often display when extolling the efficiency of the markets, that they have reliable explanations of what has driven aggregate stock markets, which they are just keeping to themselves. They can of course give examples that justify the stock price changes of some individual firms. But they cannot do this for the aggregate stock market. Over the years economists have tried to give a convincing explanation for aggregate stock price movements in terms of economic fundamentals. But no one has ever succeeded. (Akerlof and Shiller, 2009, p. 131)

A similar comparison can be made for investments in stocks in countries other than the United States, with similar conclusions.

For bond investments the picture is even bleaker. Credit Suisse researchers Dimson, Marsh, Staunton, McGinnie, and Wilmot[2] calculate the returns for bonds, before taxes and fees, for the period from 1900 to 2013.

Table 2.1 Bond real returns (1900–2013)

Country	Bond real return (%)
Switzerland	2.2
US	1.9
Japan	−1.0
Germany	−1.6

Source: Credit Suisse Global Investment Returns Yearbook, February 2014.

Table 2.1 illustrates that investing in bonds generates only limited real value. In countries such as Germany and Japan, where wars and financial crises (hyperinflation, failure of sovereign debt, etc.) transpired, significant value was destroyed.

In the above examples, we use indices as a basis for our consideration. But is it possible to achieve better results and beat these indices by investing in active managers? What are the chances of succeeding? A review by Cuthbertson, Nitzsche, and O'Sullivan[3] examined the performance of mutual funds by analyzing more than

50 studies that were published by the US and the UK between 1990 and 2010, and they report the following:

> Ex post, there are around 0–5% of top performing UK and US equity mutual funds with truly positive alpha performance (after fees) and around 20% of funds that have truly poor alpha performance with about 75% of active funds which are effectively zero alpha funds. Key driver of relative performance are load fees, expenses and turnover. (Cuthbertson, Nitzsche, and O'Sullivan, 2010, p. 91)

In other words, positive alpha which indicates that the returns are higher than a benchmark are rarely achieved in the mutual fund industry.

Fernandez and Del Campo[4] offer an even more radical example demonstrating that from 1999–2009 only 16 of the 1,117 available mutual funds in Spain (1.4 percent), with a variety of different strategies for investing in shares or bonds, generated returns above the ten-year state bond. The average return was below inflation, and only four had returns above 10 percent, with 263 showing negative returns.

TAXES, FEES, AND OTHER COSTS

In evaluating investment performance one might easily get caught up in stocks and bonds returns data, but these data alone do not tell the full story. Investors should look carefully at total returns, and real inflation-adjusted returns. A study by Thornburg Investment Management[5] calculates returns adjusted for inflation, taxes, and investment expenses – the "real" returns. The study illustrates that in the period between 1982 and 2012, the nominal return of the S&P 500 index was 10.80 percent, but after adjusting for expenses, taxes, and inflation the final return was a mere 5.79 percent (see Figure 2.4).

Figure 2.4   Nominal vs. real returns

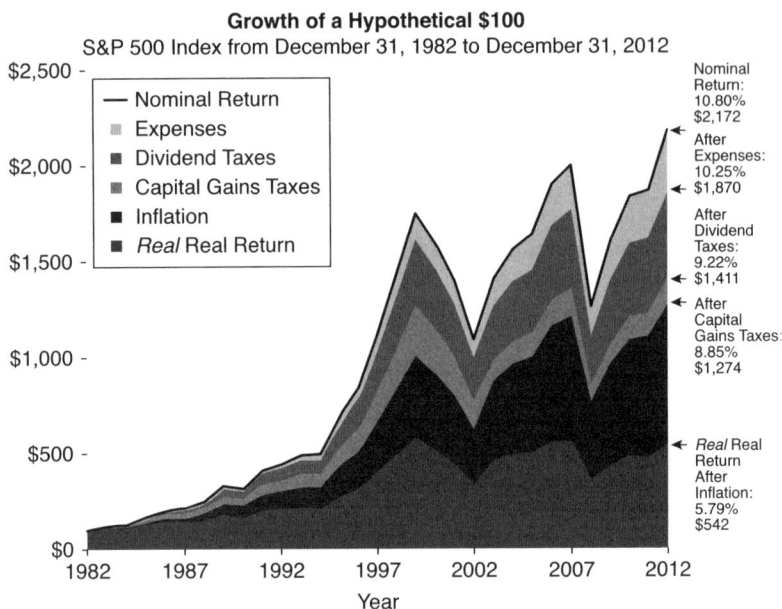

Growth of a Hypothetical $100
S&P 500 Index from December 31, 1982 to December 31, 2012

Legend:
— Nominal Return
■ Expenses
■ Dividend Taxes
■ Capital Gains Taxes
■ Inflation
■ *Real* Real Return

Nominal Return: 10.80% $2,172
After Expenses: 10.25% $1,870
After Dividend Taxes: 9.22% $1,411
After Capital Gains Taxes: 8.85% $1,274
Real Real Return After Inflation: 5.79% $542

Source: Thornburg Investment Management 2013.

THE TEMPTATION TO FOLLOW SIMPLE GRAPHS AND THE CATASTROPHIC EFFECTS OF POWER LAWS

Besides the weak returns of stocks and bonds, another important factor contributing to poor portfolio performance is that the models applied by most academicians and financial experts do not give a true picture of expected performance due to simplified models and the application of the standard deviation as a basis for returns expectation. In their popular finance textbook, *Corporate Finance*, Ross, Westerfield, and Jaffe[6] explain that with a large enough sample of stock market returns and a long enough observation period (about 1,000 years), distribution of returns would form a "Normal" bell-shaped curve as shown in Figure 2.5.

Figure 2.5   The Normal Distribution

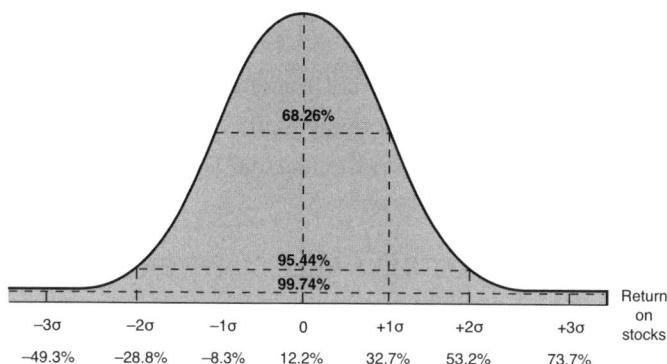

Source: Ross Stephan, Westerfield Randolph and Jaffe Jeffrey, 2010 *Corporate Finance*, 247–249.

This would be excellent news since Brealey and Myers[7] point out that "Normal Distributions can be completely defined by two numbers: one is the average or expected return (the historic mean of observed returns) and the other is the variance or standard deviation. They are the only two measures that an investor needs to consider."

However, looking at the Normal Distribution of Figure 2.5, a hypothetical investment portfolio with a historic average return of 12.2 percent could with a probability of 68.26 percent generate an investment return between −8.3 and 32.7 percent! Returns based on this commonly used "Normal Distribution" would sometimes be positive and sometimes negative across a broad performance range.

The key mathematical concept of what constitutes a Normal Distribution was developed by Carl Friedrich Gauss, considered one of the seminal mathematicians of the nineteenth century. Not surprisingly, quantitative economists of the first half of the twentieth century were keen to use Gauss's concepts to construct models for optimal portfolio construction, particularly because of its simplicity, which led to the Capital Asset Pricing Model (CAPM), optimizing return and risk, and the Modern Portfolio Theory

(MPT). As these mathematical models gained wider industry acceptance, they evolved into a marketing tool for advisors who claimed
that their advice was based on the work by Nobel prize-winning
academic researchers. Until today, many financial institutions use
this classic concept of risk management, standard deviation, and
other measurements, based on the Normal Distribution.[8]

SO IS INVESTING A BELL CURVE GAME?

The question is whether stock market returns follow a Normal Distribution. Research conducted in the late 1990s and early 2000s suggest
that the hypothesis of Normal Distribution does not conform to
many events in the financial markets. Marcus Davidsson[9] discusses
the large impact event in financial markets using comprehensive data
sets, including the daily S&P 500 from 1950 to 2010, and monthly
data from 1997 to 2010 to determine whether returns are normally
distributed. His empirical study concludes that "the daily returns for
the S&P 500 are more volatile than expected," and "both large negative and positive returns are far more frequent than predicted by the
Normal Distribution" (Davidsson, 2012, pp. 95–97).

While financial markets may follow the laws of Normal Distribution for a period of time, unanticipated events can cause significant deviations with tremendous consequences. Financial markets
during these rare events follow power laws, a kind of probability
distribution where occurrence of rare events have a much higher
probability than in a Normal Distribution.[10] Many phenomena in
other fields also follow power laws, such as magnitude of earth-
quakes in earth science and city populations in demography.

Benoit Mandelbrot,[11] an inventor of fractal geometry explains:

> Contrary to orthodoxy, price changes are very far from the bell
> curve. If they did, you should be able to run any market's price
> records through a computer, analyze the changes, and watch them

fall into the approximate "normality". ... In fact, the bell curve fits reality very poorly. From 1916 to 2003, the daily index movements of the Dow Jones Industrial Average don't spread out on graph paper like a simple bell curve. The far edges flare too high: too many big changes. Theory suggests that over that time, there should be fifty-eight days when the Dow moved more than 3.4 percent; in fact, there were 1,001. Theory predicts six days of index swings beyond 4.5 percent: in fact there were 366. And index swings of more than 7 percent should come once every 300,000 years; in fact, the twentieth century saw forty-eight such days. Truly, a calamitous era that insists on flaunting all predictions. Or, perhaps, our assumptions are wrong. Examine price records more closely, and you typically find a different kind of distribution than the bell curve: The tails do not become imperceptible but follow a power law. (Mandelbrot and Hudson, 2008, pp. 523–537)

The outliers effectively undermine the assumptions of a Normal Distribution of stock returns that form the basis for the majority of models used in the financial services industry today.

THE TREMENDOUS IMPACT OF POWER LAW EVENTS

To illustrate the magnitude of these outliers, Table 2.2 shows a few of the worst market events that resulted in great financial losses, along with their respective standard deviation.

Table 2.2   Stock market events volatility (Dow Jones index)

Stock market event (Dow Jones index)	Standard deviation σ (volatility)
Crash of October 19, 1987, NYSE	24.5
Crash of October 27, 1997	10.2
Russian Crisis August 24, 1998	7.8

Source: Puempin and Pedergnana (2008, pp. 20–21).

While standard deviation alone does not tell the whole story, these rare events are so extreme that the application of standard deviation and the probabilities used in traditional models indicate that such events should only occur in time spans that exceed the age of the universe. But these events have indeed occurred within the past 25 years, demonstrating the fallacy of financial models based on standard deviation and the Normal Distribution.

For instance, according to the Gauss Normal Distribution, the crash of 1987 (standard deviation σ 24.5) was supposed to occur only once in every 1×10^{130} years. Explicitly presented, once in every: 10,000, 000,000,000,000,000,000,000,000,000,000,000,000,000,000,000,000, 000,000,000,000,000,000,000,000,000,000,000,000,000,000,000,000, 000,000,000,000,000,000,000,000,000,000,000 years.

Since the age of the universe is 1×10^{10} years, the prevailing models suggest that such an event should not have occurred in the lifetime of the universe, and it is therefore impossible to quantify the risk factor of these events since they should never have occurred to begin with. This is yet more evidence that stock market returns do not follow the Normal Distribution and models built on this assumption are flawed.[12]

Considering the enormous magnitude such power events have, and not knowing the probability of their occurrence, what should an investor do to manage risk? In his book, *The Black Swan,* Nassim Taleb[13] calls the appearance of events that follow a power law "black swans." In Europe only white swans were known until the discovery of Australian black swans. In the investment world black swans do not follow a Normal Distribution and Taleb suggests that investors need to know the consequences of an event, even without knowing the probability of its occurrence. Taleb adds, "I don't know the odds of an earthquake, but I can imagine how San Francisco might be affected by one" (Taleb, 2010, p. 211), emphasizing the need to focus on recognizable event consequences when making decisions, rather than worrying about the probabilities. This leaves an investor with an uncertain view of the future and we discuss later how an investor can partially prepare for such events.

WHY IS THE FINANCIAL SERVICES INDUSTRY (STILL) PROMOTING STOCKS AND BONDS?

Stocks and bonds as an asset class have not generated impressive returns during the last 15 years, especially after inflation and related costs. As a consequence most investment professionals find it difficult to achieve higher returns than the risk free rate. Why then do so many advisors suggest that their clients invest predominantly in these asset classes?

Perhaps the first and main reason is tradition. The bond business goes back to Italian cities that issued the first bonds in the sixteenth century.[14] At that time the Fuggers family, a major financier of the Holy Roman Empire, developed similar financial instruments[15] and with time financiers and bankers, including the Rothschilds, attained a powerful position in the market for government securities. Bonds became a major banking activity in the nineteenth century and banks have developed a tradition of selling bonds since then.

The concept of the stock market was invented by the Dutch in the seventeenth century and stock exchanges have emerged throughout the world, with highly developed markets in Europe, the US, and Japan.[16] Banks have been actively engaged in stock transactions, advising customers on stock purchases since the invention of the stock market. And the huge and highly liquid markets of today, together with the associated trading commissions, encourage financial institutions to promote stocks and bonds. If a broker recommends buying or selling a well-capitalized stock like Google, he knows he can execute the trade immediately and without problems. The same goes for the highly liquid markets of government bonds. And today with the advent of information technology traders around the world can buy and sell these instruments with a click of a mouse, even from the comfort of their home.

Academia has also played an important role in promoting the traditional approach, most business schools and universities teach the financial models described earlier. The highly liquid markets for which complete data are available allow academicians to conduct extensive research based on statistical methods that were published in the 1950s, 1960s, and 1970s.[17] And in the 1990s the fields of finance and economics were glorified as a good number of their Nobel prize winners were academicians originally trained in physics and mathematics, which enabled them to simplify the world according to quantitative models. However, as the test of time has challenged these financial models, business schools have begun questioning the validity of the models that form the basis for majority of the investment practices today.

Finally, it is important to keep in mind that the business model of financial services institutions depends in great part on brokerage fees to maximize profits, even though these fees lower investor returns. Moreover, the financial services industry has invested extensive resources in IT and other systems, which generate revenue only when used on a large scale in liquid and voluminous markets such as stocks and bonds.

CHALLENGES FACING NEAR-TERM PERFORMANCE

While it is impossible to predict with certainty what will happen to investment performance in the coming years, it is reasonable to assume that massive quantitative easing, as central banks basically print money, with low interest rates as a consequence, will have a negative impact on bond performance. John Mauldin,[18] president of Millennium Wave Investments and co-author of the highly praised book *Endgame* puts it bluntly:

> The muddle through economy has important implications for inves-
> tors. Investors will have to adjust to this new reality. ... For longer-term
> investors, this change of paradigm means that achieving consistent
> solid returns becomes even more difficult. ... That's pretty much it.
> This is not a problem we can grow ourselves out of in the next few

years. ... We are going to have to deal with the pain. It will be the pain of reduced returns on traditional stock market investments, eventually a lower dollar against most currencies (other than the euro, the pound, and the yen), low returns on bonds, ... lower corporate profits over the long term, and a very slow-growth environment. (Mauldin and Tepper, 2013, p. 86 and 206, 207)

Bill Gross,[19] the founder of PIMCO, with assets of US \$2 trillion under management as of November 2013 asks: "What then is an investor to do? In a New Normal economy where lenders dance to the Blue Danube instead of the Lindy how should we move our own feet? Carefully, I suppose, and with recognition that historic returns are just that – historic. ... Returns from both stocks and bonds will be stunted. ... The age of inflation is upon us, which typically provides a headwind, not a tailwind, to securities prices – both stocks and bonds" (Gross, 2012, p. 3).

CONCLUSION: WHAT TO EXPECT FROM TRADITIONAL INVESTMENT CONCEPTS

An investor who follows the recommendations of financial advisors that focus on stocks and bonds may in some cases be able to preserve capital. But to build significant wealth, an investor must strive for considerably higher annual returns, and this requires a different approach. Keeping in mind that investments always take place in a dynamic social system, it is essential to understand concepts of strategy and their implications for developing a sound investment approach.

Chapter 3

THE INVESTOR BACK AT THE CORE OF INVESTING: LESSONS FROM A CFO – PART 2

Martin's wealth creation succeeded only when he changed his investment approach fundamentally and became a strategic investor. Having abandoned attempts to generate wealth through quoted stocks and bonds, he began talking to friends about their investment strategies. He consulted successful entrepreneurs on their approach to investing and a previous employer who was a respected investor was generous in sharing advice. In the meantime since he could not yet make a living through investing alone, he continued to work as a CFO to generate income.

Martin realized that he needed to develop an investment portfolio beyond stocks and bonds. He diligently studied various asset classes, such as hedge funds and private equity, and began to concentrate his investments in small cap companies and real estate while exploring direct investments in privately held companies. He especially liked the idea of direct investments since he was already familiar with many cutting-edge management techniques, and from personal experience as a manager he was confident that he could create value in the companies he would invest in. With his ability in approaching people, he began to build a network to identify unquoted companies in need of funds that might also benefit from his management know-how. He made a special effort to surround himself with a network of older, more experienced and intelligent people to observe their decision making. He read the latest management literature on mergers and acquisitions, valuation methodologies, due diligence, and other methodologies used in evaluating and executing direct investments. He regularly attended symposia and conferences where he made promising contacts whom he might approach as a direct investor.

Following diligent preparation and careful review of the market, Martin identified his first direct investment in 2000. He learned about the opportunity through a consultant who told him about a business owner eager to retire from a company that sold specialty batteries, including buttons for micro-electronic devices and hearing aids. The consultant, who wanted to run the business himself, lacked sufficient cash and was searching to find another investor to support him. Martin, he believed, would be an excellent partner given his business expertise and ability to provide valuable input in the development of the business.

Martin decided to invest in the company after careful review of the opportunity, explaining:

> This business clearly was at the beginning of a strong life cycle. Due to the extremely loud music and sound in earphones and disco shops, more and more (younger) people would have to buy hearing aids. I realized that this would guarantee a strong growth market. Moreover, because the life cycle of a hearing aid battery is only about 15 hours, demand would be continuous. It was just a question of finding the right sales model.

Because the owner wanted to sell quickly and had not yet con-tacted other investors, the price for the business appeared reasonable, and Martin invested US $400,000 in the venture.

As in any direct investment there were many risks to manage and Martin decided to focus on areas where he could add value. Much of the company's future success would stem from a new direct distribu-tion strategy via the Internet, creating a major competitive advantage. Prior to distribution via the Internet, hearing aid users had to go to specialty stores where they paid high prices for a limited selection. On the Internet, customers could order with one click, at a better price, from a wide variety of specialty batteries, and with delivery directly to their homes. With Martin's guidance and successful implementation of this strategy, the company began to flourish and in the second year it paid a dividend of $75,000 on his investment.

With his remaining cash and new dividends, Martin searched for other investment opportunities in small privately owned companies that conformed to his investment criteria: the companies had to be lower tech, with easy-to-understand products, have low capital inten-sity, and a minimal need for highly qualified personnel. He delib-erately decided not to consider turnaround situations and instead turned his focus to what he understood and had a competitive edge in, as this was the best way he could add value.

Martin's second direct investment opportunity came through a small-business lawyer who told him that an entrepreneur was look-ing for an investor to expand his business of dry cleaning shops. After due diligence, Martin concluded that there was a growing market for the dry cleaning business as younger singles opted for convenience. With relatively low capital intensity the fixed costs were minimal, and given the broad customer base Martin concluded that risk was also limited. The owner trusted Martin's management know-how and wanted his input, offering him an exclusive investment option at a fair price.

Martin decided to invest US $500,000 in his second business and was able to add value by offering useful suggestions to his new partner. Following Martin's advice, the original owner moved several stores to locations with higher customer traffic, and to guarantee one-day service they extended store hours to provide "morning drop off for evening pickup." The company introduced new services such as offering package deals to nearby hotels. According to Martin, "The investor has to look beyond financials. I discovered that I had to take care of processes, organization, and other management issues. As an outsider, I was able to provide fresh ideas to improve the business."

Over time, Martin developed a systematic strategy of pursuing direct investments in privately held small- and mid-sized companies. Through his growing network of lawyers, auditors, merger and acquisition specialists, and other professionals, he was continually on the lookout for opportunities to investigate. According to Martin:

> Once the finance community knew I was willing to consider investing in certain well-defined companies they sent me all kinds of proposals. I knew I had to stick to the investment criteria I had developed: potential companies for investment had to be lower tech, with easily understandable products, low capital intensity, and sound cash flows who could benefit from my know-how and allow me to contribute to the success of the company. Otherwise, I would have lost my focus and increased the risk. The expansion of my investments had to grow step by step.

With several successful investments in his portfolio, Martin was generating a satisfactory income providing consulting services, mostly to the companies he invested in. This enabled him to give up his job as a CFO and to dedicate all his time to supporting the growth of the companies he invested in. The additional freedom enabled him to devote further attention to his portfolio and to diversify his investments into other asset classes. Aware that there are always unexpected events, he decided not to put all his money into a single investment or asset class and, in consultation with a friend who was a hedge fund expert, he invested approximately 15 percent of his wealth in ETFs[1] and a broadly diversified portfolio of hedge funds. This strategy led to reducing his overall risk while still achieving an annual return of 5-to-10 percent.

As the father of three children, Martin felt it was prudent to place some of his holdings in highly secure assets: he owned his original house as a safe investment, bought an upscale condominium, and built a comfortable cash position. He purchased life insurance to protect his family and, as a hedge against inflation, invested 5 percent of his net worth in gold and other precious metals.

Although the battery company experienced some problems, in general Martin's focus on direct investments succeeded. With his extensive knowledge as both a board member and a consultant, he contributed significantly to the prosperity of the companies he invested in. His evolving network proved a fruitful source of suggestions for new investment opportunities at reasonable prices. His direct investments not only generated good returns but he also achieved tax advantages and low transaction and custody fees. By 2012 he had increased his personal wealth by several million dollars in direct investments, with a net worth of over US $10 million.

Martin is now well-known in his business community as a direct investor and new investment proposals are pitched to him on a regular basis. Reflecting on his success he admitted that had he listened to his banker and invested only in stocks and bonds he would never have prospered as he did.[2] Only when he became a strategic investor did things begin to change for him, and his success stemmed from application of fundamental strategic guidelines, described in later chapters, and principles that support effective wealth creation.

Martin had to create his own path. He began with an analysis of his strengths and competencies, and he developed a network to gain access to investments where he could use those skills. He systematically improved his knowledge and experience, stayed focused avoiding certain risks, and cut his losses early when the situation called for it. Participation on the boards of the companies he invested in was key. "Direct investments" he confided, "force you to do a thorough analysis, to engage yourself personally with deep and continuous participation in the business. Because you have a direct relationship to the company, you can also identify new opportunities and trends in the market."

Chapter 4
THE ESSENCE OF STRATEGY

THE BATTLE OF SALAMIS

Creating wealth through investments is a strategic challenge where key elements of strategic principles are implicated. To illustrate we use a fifth century BC example from a military strategy which helped the weaker side achieve victory over a much stronger opponent.

The Persian Achamenids Empire in the fifth century BC was "governing a territory larger than all the ancient empires, including even Rome's" (Chua, 2009, p.4).[1] Under Darius the Great the empire reached from India to Greece and his son Xerxes (519–465 BC) had ambitious plans to expand the empire to the Atlantic Ocean to control the entire Mediterranean region and the European continent. However, a few small Greek states blocked the way to the West, and Xerxes' immediate objective was to conquer the Greek states.

In 480 BC Xerxes attempted to invade the Greek mainland with a tremendous army, and to reach the mainland he first had to destroy a fleet of about 200 Greek vessels that protected the homeland. Xerxes was optimistic. His navy consisted of over 600 heavy triremes (rowing vessels), far superior to the Greek fleet. He planned a naval engagement convinced that victory would come when the Greek vessels, intimidated by the Persian naval fleet, withdraw to the Gulf of Salamis.

The Greek commander Themistocles was keenly aware that he was outnumbered by at least three to one, and his generals argued about whether the Greeks should go into battle at all. But Themistocles persevered and developed a battle strategy that convinced his commanders to take on the enemy.

Themistocles' strategy consisted of several strands. First, he made certain that all the other Greek City States supported him, not an easy task considering they had been fighting each other for decades. Once he managed to obtain their support, he next had to decide where to engage in battle. On the open seas the Persians could deploy their forces fully against his much smaller fleet. Therefore Themistocles decided to lure the Persians into the bay of Salamis where Xerxes could not make full use of his stronger fleet due to the geographical limitations of the bay. Themistocles also knew his Greek ships were faster and more maneuverable than the Persian fleet, which would allow him to attack the right flank of the Persian fleet with speed to break their battle formation. Finally, the Greek ships were equipped with an infantry that excelled in close combat so, aided by the faster ships, the Greek infantry could board the Persian ships quickly and conquer their crews.[2]

Themistocles' strategic objective was clear: he had to destroy the Persian fleet to prevent the occupation of Greece. The most important element of his strategy was *the clever deployment of limited resources (vessels and troops)* which enabled him to defeat the Persian fleet and shape world history.

The deployment of resources is at the core of any strategy and Themistocles had to consider several factors. First, he had to use his *strengths* and *competences* by putting his fastest ships and best infantry in position to attack the Persians' right flank.

Figure 4.1 The Battle of Salamis

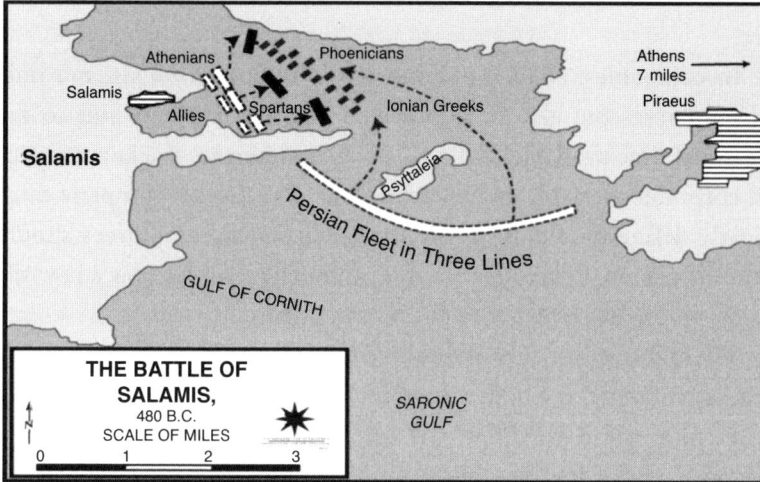

Source: "The Battle of Salamis." Wikipedia, The Free Encyclopedia. Wikimedia Foundation, Inc. March 14, 2014.

Second, he used the *geographic layout* of the bay of Salamis to give him a significant *opportunity* because his enemy could not fully deploy its forces. Third, by using his faster ships, Themistocles could use *time* to his advantage. The Persians were not able to build up their superiority in time and so – call it *right timing* – the Greeks were able to defeat the Persians ship by ship.

Finally, the *coalition* he created with other Greek City States ensured that even with considerably fewer forces Themistocles' limited resources (ships, troops, etc.) were sufficient to achieve victory.

THE CORE ELEMENTS OF STRATEGY

The fundamental task of a strategist is to make *optimal use of available resources to achieve an objective*. Resources can be human (such as the soldiers at Salamis) or physical (such as ships). Similarly, in developing a wealth-building strategy, the investor must efficiently deploy his or her resources: time, finances, networks, IT systems, etc.

In companies, as in the military, key resources consist not only of employees but also factories, equipment, computers and so on. Personal time available to managers and employees is a key resource in corporate strategy, and to achieve its objectives a company must clearly define the fields of activity managers and employees should concentrate on. Financial resources and networks also play a key role in corporate strategy.

The higher the quality of resources (at Salamis, fast ships and highly trained infantry) the better the chance of achieving strategic success. Therefore, the *capabilities and competences* of available resources become crucial for every strategy. They must be built to constitute real strengths the strategist can rely on. Just as in the military, and in business, the strategic investor must ensure that he or she has developed unique strengths and core competences for deployment.

Why is this so important? In military or corporate strategy it is obvious that the army or the company has to deal with opponents or competitors. As the general must conquer his enemy, the company CEO must develop a strategy for success over the competition. But what about investing?

At first glance, competition is not a central concern in investing. The investor just places an order with his broker and expects that, in liquid markets, the order will be executed. A closer look, however, reveals that competition is actually an integral part of the investment landscape. With large cap stocks, for example, companies are followed by hundreds of analysts, each of whom strives to do better research than the competitors to determine whether a stock is undervalued or overvalued. This insight provides a competitive advantage to the investor who has access to the information because he, his company, or its customers can make more accurate investment decisions. The competitive nature of investing is even more evident when we examine investment bank auctions of privately held companies, where private investors, corporate investors, and private equity firms are in direct competition with each other for an acquisition.

A third element of strategy is that it always takes place within an *environment*. At Salamis the environment consisted of the geography south of Athens – the Salamis peninsula. But geography is only one element in military strategy. A variety of other environmental factors, such as weather, technology, or even pandemics, can play a major role. Just as Themistocles used these environmental factors in his strategic decisions, strategic investors must take account of environmental factors such as economic cycles, demographic trends, technological advancements and, most importantly, market factors.

To recap, the following elements constitute the essence of strategy:

1. Core strategic decisions involve the deployment of resources available to the strategist, including:
   - Human resources (e.g.: soldiers in military strategy, employees in management strategy, personal time in a private investor's strategy)
   - Material resources (e.g.: weapons in military strategy, factories in corporate strategy, IT resources in a private investor's strategy)
   - Financial resources (e.g.: cash to pay soldiers and purchase weapons in military strategy, working capital in management strategy, liquidity for investments in a private investors' strategy).

   The strategist must fully understand the strengths and weaknesses of the available resources and mobilize them effectively.
2. In any strategy, opponents or competitors interact with the strategist. In military strategy, this is the enemy. In management

strategy it is the competition. In finance strategy the opponents are usually countless other investors all planning to invest under attractive conditions, for the highest returns and lowest possible risk. The strategist must carefully consider these opponents in his or her strategic decision-making.

3. Strategy takes place in an environment. In military strategy this environment may include geography, topography, climate conditions and so on. In management strategy external factors such as economic and technological developments, demographic trends and, of course, market developments play important roles. In investment strategy, environmental factors include the state of the economy, interest rates, debt market liquidity, technological advancements, and demographic trends. These environmental factors and developments must be integrated in the strategic decision-making.

STRATEGIC PRINCIPLES: UNIVERSAL LAWS OF LIFE

From a systems point of view strategic principles apply in all *dynamic, complex social systems*. The core elements of strategy found in the military, management, and finance sectors are present in many other fields, including chess, competitive sports, and social contests. In these systems, success depends on a strategically correct deployment of available resources, which leads to an interesting question: are there generic rules or principles the strategist can apply when deploying available resources?

Many such principles have been developed, originally for military strategy. One of the first collections of such principles can be found in Sun Tzu's book (ca. 500 BC)[3] and in General Tan Daoji's work (ca. AD 400).[4] In *The Art of War,*[5] Sun Tzu, the Chinese military general, strategist and philosopher, espouses principles similar to those essential for strategic investing, such as building on strengths, avoiding weaknesses and using networks for access to valuable, reliable, and timely information (analogous to spy networks in the military).

In European literature, *The Peloponnesian War* by Thucydides (ca. 431–404 BC)[6] is another seminal work with valuable insights into strategy. Several centuries later, the military campaigns of Julius Caesar against the Gallic tribes (ca. 58 BC to 50 BC) were superbly documented. Sidney Schoeffler, founder of the Strategic Planning Institute in Cambridge (Massachusetts) once confided to one of our co-authors, "If you want to learn about strategy, you must read *The Gallic War* by Julius Caesar" because of the many fundamental strategic rules it incorporates. Other classic works include *Précis de l'Art de la Guerre*[7] by Antoine-Henri Jomini (1779–1869), and Carl Philipp Gottlieb von Clausewitz's (1780–1831) *Vom Kriege*[8] which highlight the importance of concentration of forces.

Erich von Mannstein (1887–1973),[9] Bernard Law Montgomery (1887–1976),[10] and Basil Liddell Hart (1895–1970)[11] presented new principles on strategy in the twentieth century. Hart stresses the principle of the "indirect approach," stating that "in strategy the longest way around is often the shortest way there. A direct approach to the object exhausts the attacker and hardens the resistance by compression, whereas an indirect approach loosens the defender's hold by upsetting his balance" (Hart, 1943).

In modern literature on warfare, we find additional principles such as surprise and simplicity. The British Defence Doctrine[12] suggests, "Surprise is the consequence of shock and confusion induced by the deliberate or incidental introduction of the unexpected" (British Defence Doctrine, 2011, pp. 2–5). Other important related elements such as energy (the power with which strategic actions are executed) have also been discussed in detail.[13]

Applications of strategic principles in management science have evolved since the 1960s, with a broad range of books describing principles for success and effective deployment of resources. Some of the major works include Bradley Gale's *The PIMS Principles*,[14] Michael

Figure 4.2   Strategy framework, five forces

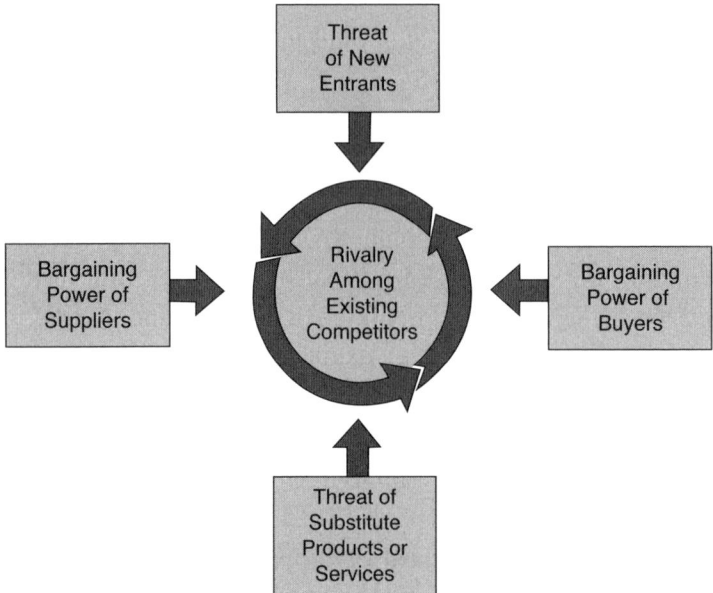

Source: Michael Porter, 1997, How Competitive Forces Shape Strategy.

Porter's *Competitive Strategy*,[15] and Cuno Puempin's *The Essence of Strategy*,[16] and *How World Class Companies became World Class*.[17]

A number of influential frameworks have been developed to guide corporate strategy. In his five forces model, Michael Porter establishes a framework that has shaped a generation of business practices and started a revolution in the field of strategy. According to this framework the extended rivalry that results from the five forces defines an industry's structure and shapes the nature of competitive interaction within the industry.[18]

Until now finance literature has lacked a useful framework for application of strategy to investments. In the following chapter we propose a new framework that can aid an investor in developing and deploying a robust strategy for wealth creation.

Chapter 5

THE EMPOWERED INVESTOR: A NEW PARADIGM OF INVESTING

A FRAMEWORK FOR STRATEGIC WEALTH CREATION

The literature on strategy deals with dozens of different principles. Some are general, like the advice to "build on strengths," and others apply to only a specific field such as strategic management. In this book, we have chosen to concentrate on key principles that are crucial for wealth creation. We aim to empower the investor in developing and successfully implementing his or her unique investment strategy using a new strategic framework presented in this chapter.

One of the key success factors in the battle of Salamis was Themistocles' strategy of leveraging on the strengths of the Greek army. This concept of building on strengths can be found throughout history and is a central element of our framework for strategic wealth creation. Another decisive principle on the battle field was taking advantage of the opportunity the geographical landscape offered. Exploitation of opportunities in the investment landscape is likewise a decisive element of strategic investing. Every investment activity is faced with

numerous potential threats and risks that must be mitigated effectively. Handling threats and risks is thus the third principle of the
framework.

The effective use of networks as a strategic imperative was evident
in our interviews with successful investors, many of whom emphasized the development of networks as a key principle in their investment strategy. Effective use of networks is a fourth principle of our
framework.

The three remaining principles of the framework relate to the
evolution of complex systems. In his book *Energon: The Hidden
Secret*,[1] the biologist Hans Hass argues that evolutionarily successful
species have advantages in three areas:

- they are more differentiated, having found a niche and opti-
  mally adapted to it[2]
- they are more (energy-) efficient since they use less energy than
  their opponents to survive;[3] and
- they are efficient in the time dimension, mainly by quickly
  adapting to new environmental conditions.

These three elements were also recognized in strategic management.
Cuno Puempin, one of our co-authors, has shown that differentiation, efficiency, and timing must be considered in the process of strategic management.[4] This process consists of four stages:

1. Information analysis
2. Strategy development
3. Strategy implementation
4. Strategic controlling.

The three elements of differentiation, efficiency, and timing essential for living systems, and companies are equally essential for wealth
creation. The strategist must analyze which fields of activity have

the most potential for differentiation and efficiency gains (i.e. cost reductions), and the timing with which strategic moves shall be implemented.

The seven strategic principles are thus incorporated in the framework for wealth creation:

- The first core principle is building on strengths. The strategist must ask which strengths he can build on and deploy resources to leverage existing strengths.
- A good strategy exploits opportunities, and identifying unique opportunities is essential. The strategy must define what resources the investor should devote toward exploiting attractive opportunities.
- Networks and coalitions play a major role in successful investment strategies. By deploying resources, the investor must exploit existing networks and build new ones to successfully implement the strategy.
- Successful strategies differ from the mainstream. A strategist should try to be different from the majority of competitors by applying an indirect approach (explained later). Differentiation requires hard work and deploying manpower, time, and financial resources.
- Every investor confronts threats and risks. A sound evaluation of these elements becomes an important ingredient of a successful strategy, with sufficient time and funding devoted to their prevention.
- Good strategies fit into overall market trends and cycles. Correct timing of a strategy is crucial and should be carefully assessed with investment of sufficient time and other resources.
- Finally, a successful strategy achieves its objectives efficiently, ensuring that the objectives are in harmony with the available resources.

These seven elements are, of course, not isolated but tightly intercon-
nected. For instance, networks can be used for identifying opportunities or for building strengths/competences.

This new framework of strategic wealth creation is presented in
Figure 5.1.

Figure 5.1   The framework of strategic wealth creation

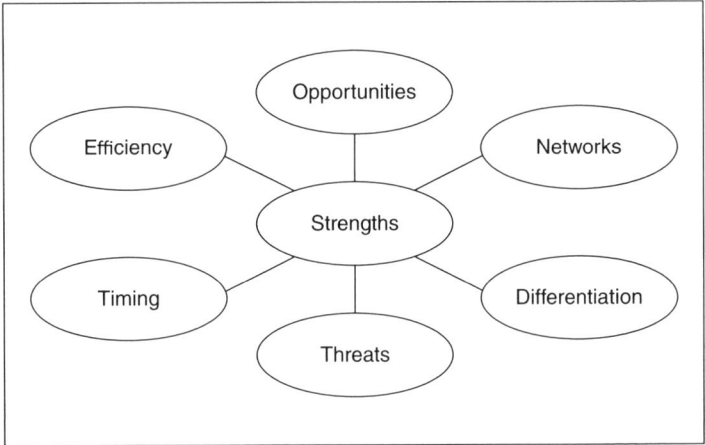

Source: Authors.

In the rest of this chapter we discuss the seven elements of the
framework, and in later chapters we elaborate on how the framework
can be applied by the strategic investor. At this point we emphasize
that our research has clearly shown that an investor can only build
wealth by applying a strategic approach, and the framework presented
here has been designed to aid in developing a sound strategy.

STRENGTHS: THE INVESTOR AT THE CORE OF INVESTMENT STRATEGY

The importance of strengths

Strategic teachings emphasize the concept of building a strategy on
the strengths of the organization or individual. From a strategic point

of view, strength is a special competency or capability that makes the organization or person superior to others and provides a sound basis for achieving these competences. Military strategists have known this principle for millennia. Sun Tzsu stressed the importance of strengths in the sixth century BC. Building on strengths was also a key element in the success of Rome: "The size, strength and organization of their [Rome's] infantry force wouldn't be equaled again for another thousand years... The core of Rome's military strength lay in the professionalism of their heavy infantry. A force that was organized and reorganized as it evolved and adapted to survive the assaults of its mortal enemies, and conquer the Western world"[5] (Ancient Military, 2010).

In corporate strategy, Apple Inc., under Steve Jobs, demonstrated a special strength in innovating integrated computers, tablets, and smartphones where the company controls hardware, software, and related business activities, such as the Apple stores.[6] Apple's strength has been shown in its devotion to research and development that has kept the Apple innovation system operating at full capacity.[7]

Although the concept of building on strengths has been discussed at length in military literature, it was not until the 1980s that several publications put strengths at the core of strategic thinking.

One of the first publications to emphasize strengths was Cuno Puempin's *The Essence of Corporate Strategy* in 1987. Later, The Boston Consulting Group promoted the concept of "Competing on Capabilities: The New Rules of Corporate Strategy."[8]

In a 1990 article in *Harvard Business Review*, "The Core Competences of the Corporation," Hamel and Prahalad gained wide acceptance for their presentation of organizational core competencies as the organization's major value-creating skills, capabilities, and resources that determine its competitiveness. Hamel and Prahalad propose that "Core Competencies are the wellspring of new business development. They should constitute the focus for the strategy at the corporate level"[9] (Hamel and Prahalad, 1990, p. 14).

Over the last two decades Audi has demonstrated this concept superbly by building on its unique strengths. Some 25 years ago, in a workshop with one of our authors, the executive board of Audi defined the key strengths the company would build upon. Audi already had considerable strengths in technology but the company had not exploited them systematically. For instance, Audi still sold several models that did not incorporate its more advanced technologies.

The then Chief Technology Officer, Ferdinand Piech (later chairman of Volkswagen), helped propel strategic decision-making in Audi, and it was decided that the company's technological strengths should be at the heart of Audi's strategy, acknowledged by the slogan *Vorsprung durch Technik* (Advantage through Technology). Since then, Audi has concentrated on producing the most advanced cars from a technological standpoint. Technology is thus Audi's central strength that helps it generate outstanding financial results: a profit of 11.03 percent in 2012,[10] making it one of the most profitable car producers worldwide.[11]

The central strategic principle of building on strengths is always the same, be it in the military, business, wealth creation, or in other complex, dynamic social systems that evolve in a competitive environment where superior capabilities or competences are a core success factor.[12] As investments take place in complex, dynamic social systems, the strategic investor should apply this principle and identify where he already has unique strengths or which fields of investment he could build his strengths in to achieve success.

Why is this so important?

- First, strong competences enable the strategist to make the right investment decisions. For instance, if an investor such as Martin (in the Chapter 1) defines direct investments as the core of his strategy, and if he has a strength (outstanding know-how) in this field, he can evaluate investment opportunities more accurately and will make fewer mistakes that could lead to losses. And since considerable know-how is essential, strengths should be continually improved.

- Second, in dynamic social systems an investor will always face competition. A real estate investor considering an investment in a property will encounter other investors also intending to invest in the same property. So the investor needs outstanding skills in evaluation, negotiation, and related activities, competences that will enable him to build a portfolio of properties at fair prices.

- The third reason is related to the "economy of forces."[13] As we will see later under the heading of "efficiency," every strategy has an economic dimension that must be realized at a reasonable cost. These costs will be lower when the strategist already has some strengths or know-how with regard to the strategy. If there are no such competences available the strategist must build them from scratch, leading to higher costs.

- Finally, investing without core competences is a very risky endeavor with a high probability of failing.

Why are strengths neglected in finance literature?

Surprisingly, investor strengths have mostly been neglected in finance literature. This is perhaps due to the evolution of finance theory over the last century where capital market theory was developed by quantitative-oriented economists who promoted mathematical model building (Modern Portfolio Theory and Capital Market Pricing Theory). The objective of these models was to define optimal capital allocation decisions,[14] and investment decisions were seen only as the allocation of funds to different asset classes, mostly from a short- or mid-term perspective. Considering that strengths are a qualitative dimension, they did not find a place in quantitative models, and quantitative analysis came to define investment decisions rather than the core competencies of the investor. Economists

preferred using homogenous "rational agents" (investors) to facilitate their modeling efforts, neglecting the fact that investors have
different skills, preferences, and amounts of capital to deploy. As
such, the obsession with quantification has overridden all qualitative criteria such as strengths, differentiation, networks, and opportunities, replacing them with quantitative concepts such as standard
deviation and backward-looking analytic models.

There is also a cultural issue emanating from the quantitative
economic tradition of some leading universities, causing modern
finance to follow a mapped path leading to more and more sophisticated mathematical models. Some academicians live in ivory towers
and consider few outside ideas (such as strategic thinking). It took
the financial crisis of 2008 for the limitations of the quantitative
approach to become evident, and many investors including Warren
Buffet began questioning the quantitative approach. Buffet's caution
to "beware of geeks bearing formulas"[15] began a viral circulation in
2009, and new ideas that take a critical perspective on quantitative
financial models such as Nassim Taleb's "black swan"[16] have now
been accepted.

How to build strengths

We look now at another investor, Uli, originally a journalist for
a leading Swiss finance publication through which he was well
connected to Swiss politics.[17] Uli was also a board member of a
leading elevator company and was instrumental in establishing the
first joint venture between China and the West. Due to his special
connections to China, Uli was named the Swiss ambassador to China
in 1985.

When he became ambassador, Uli already had many strengths
with regard to China based on his business activities and his interest
in Chinese history and culture. During his time as ambassador, he
started to build a network of leading Chinese contemporary artists

and began to acquire their paintings while at the same time extending his network to Chinese business leaders. On his return to Switzerland in 1998, Uli had unique strengths at his disposal:

- Knowledge of Chinese history and culture.
- Know-how and expertise as a businessman.
- Networks of Chinese business leaders and artists.

A passion for certain investment objects can be a defining strength, and Uli's passion for contemporary Chinese art was instrumental in his developing a strategy that enabled him to build one of the world's most valuable collections of contemporary Chinese art.

In almost all our interviews with successful investors, the importance of building on strengths was reconfirmed. Dominique, a strategic investor in the field of medical technology was the head of international sales at Sulzer Medica before he became a private investor in the field. Urs, a CEO of McDonald's Switzerland, was involved in real estate activities and he used this competence for his focus strategy after leaving McDonalds. Rainer, an assistant professor of mathematics at the University of California at Berkeley used his passion for mathematics when he developed a new hedge fund concept. In all these cases the strength of the investor was built over a long period of time, in previous job responsibilities, and became the core of the investment strategy.

Where can strengths be built?

The fact is, many of us do not really know our strengths. Donald O. Clifton, cited by the American Psychological Association as the father of Strengths Psychology and the grandfather of Positive Psychology, was asked a few months before his death in 2003 what he thought the greatest discovery in more than 30 years of leadership research was. Clifton responded, "A leader needs to know his strengths as a carpenter knows his tools, or as a physician knows the instruments at her disposal. *What great leaders have in common is that each truly knows his or her strengths – and can call on the right strength at the right time.*"[18]

Therefore, a strategist's central task is to analyze his or her personal strengths in the fields where the investor already has special capabilities or know-how.

Other factors affect personal investment strategy. Some investors choose a strategy related to their hobby, or to a field where they already have a passion. Their personal affinity to a field of investment forms an excellent basis for building strengths. Another criterion for investing is access to networks, a valuable strength on which to build a strategy.

Knowing one's actual strengths is only part of the equation. The strategist must also think about potential strengths and identify fields where strengths can be built. It is always advisable to build strengths where there are attractive opportunities. Uli, for example, made direct investments in China because he had special strengths related to that country, but equally important was that China promised strong growth opportunities.

Opportunities are related to cycles, and it is advisable to build strengths in a field at the beginning of a strong life cycle. In the late 1980s, a medical doctor, one of our interviewees, was visiting Georgia (then part of the Soviet Union) and fell in love with the beauty of the country. He visited the country on many additional trips and by the 1990s, when Georgia became independent, he already had a network of contacts there. Against the recommendations of friends in his Rotary Club, he decided to invest his savings in new food companies in Georgia and was able to exploit the impressive growth cycle of the country after 2000, achieving impressive returns on his investments. He built his strengths at a time when there was almost no competition from other investors in the country.

Concentrate!

Building strengths or competences is a key success factor for an investment strategy and therefore for wealth creation. But the question remains, how can you build strengths that allow you to build a fortune?

In his thought provoking book, *Outliers*,[19] Malcolm Gladwell tells a story about the Beatles when they were still unknown in the early sixties. Gladwell pinpoints one reason why the Beatles became the number one band in the world – they practiced day and night, achieving a high standard with their music. They did not play jazz in the morning, waltz in the afternoon and beat in the evening, but concentrated on their own new style. The point Gladwell makes (not only with the Beatles but also with other examples) is that you can only achieve outstanding capabilities and competences when you invest a tremendous amount of time to build your strengths. Gladwell's research shows that outliers usually spend more than 10,000 hours practicing. This equals 1,250 eight-hour days or four-to-five years of hard, intensive work!

It is our conviction that this rule also applies to successful strategic investors. To build strengths an investor must concentrate on a relatively narrow field of investment. The more focused the investor is with his or her time, the better the potential outcome. Therefore, only a limited number of strengths should be built or applied, otherwise resources become spread across too many activities with only marginal results.

We can see the close relationship between strengths and the necessity to concentrate forces. In strategy teachings, the idea of concentration of forces plays a central role. Henry Ford used this principle with his ModelT strategy. Making a point about concentrating his forces, Ford said: "You can have any color car so long as it's black."[20] Ford produced a single model in a single color, an extreme example of a strategy of concentration of forces.[21]

Of course, the principle of concentration of an investor's forces contradicts the philosophy of modern finance where diversification plays a central role. The key point here is that with diversification it may be possible to achieve average results, perhaps even the preservation of wealth. But it is not possible to create real wealth this way. Building wealth through strategic investing is only possible by building outstanding competences and strengths through concentration of forces.

Many successful investors have recognized and applied this idea. John Maynard Keynes encouraged investors to build a concentrated investment portfolio, suggesting that an investor makes only 20 key investments in his lifetime.[22] Warren Buffett follows a similar strategy,[23] noting that "wide diversification is only required when investors do not understand what they are doing."[24]

Assign resources

Investors must devote a tremendous amount of time, perhaps the most important resource, to build strong competences, but there are other resources. Time cannot be invested in a vacuum. Information is a resource and the investor must build an information system based on the strengths he or she focuses on.

Financial expenditure is another obvious resource. If you use your time to improve your competences, you usually have to spend money, be it on further education, purchasing research reports, and travelling, or other expenses related to strengthening your competences. When an investor is just starting to implement a strategy, and when only a small amount of cash is available, it takes courage to accept these costs and to spend money on these necessities.

Other resources include the time of professionals that are hired by wealthier investors, and family wealth management offices (family offices), who employ investment professionals to contribute to building strategic strengths.

Focus on allocation of resources

Resources can only be used on one activity at a time. During a gathering attended by one of our co-authors, Roger Federer, the Swiss tennis player ranked world No. 1 by the Association of Tennis Professionals in 2012 said, "At the age of fourteen I was already quite a good tennis player. But I was also a very good player on a Basel soccer team. In this situation my parents and I realized that every minute I played soccer was not available for tennis training. Therefore I had to take a decision, and it was for tennis. I even left my soccer club. Looking back, this decision was not so bad."[25]

The same rule counts for the strategic investor. There is always a trade-off between assigning a resource to certain strengths or to other fields of investment, as Martin explains:

> After having taken the strategic decision to concentrate on direct investments I still got investment proposals submitted to me by banks. Sometimes these proposals looked quite attractive. But I always asked myself whether I should use my time to improve my strengths in the field of direct investments or whether I should accept the bank proposals. Because I had a clear strategy, I knew that I had to concentrate on my direct investments and build on these strengths. I often declined invitations, even at the risk of causing someone to become angry with me.

Because resources can only be used one at a time, the number of strengths that can be built up is limited. The more strengths you try to build, the more difficult it becomes to follow Malcolm Gladwell's 10,000 hours rule!

Be aware of risks

Since concentration of forces can sometimes be risky, the rules of risk management we describe later in this chapter are vitally important. We suggest investing a limited part of one's wealth in uncorrelated asset classes to diversify because unexpected "black swan" events can harm even the best strategy.

But should the investor also build competences in these other asset classes? The answer is a clear no. The objective of diversification is to preserve capital and not to build wealth. Therefore, an investor can rely on investment proposals from his bank or other financial advisors, although the amount allocated to this diversification should be limited to only a part of the investor's assets.

OPPORTUNITIES: SOURCES OF WEALTH CREATION

Exploiting opportunities is a central principle in strategy. In military strategy, opportunities are often related to special features of the landscape or other conditions in the environment, such as the weather. In the example of the battle of Salamis, Themistocles used the opportunity offered by the landscape in the form of the peninsula of Salamis to hide and prevent Xerxes from deploying the full strength of his forces.

Likewise in corporate strategy, there are many examples of successful exploitation of opportunities. Starbucks identified an opportunity in the trend for Italian coffee and built an extraordinary corporate strategy to exploit it. In inventing the iPhone, Apple used the opportunity offered by technological innovation in the area of microelectronics and information technology. Toyota exploited the social trend related to increased awareness of the environment by bringing hybrid automobiles to market. And the Swiss watch-making industry is exploiting the increased buying power of the Asian middle class to boost its exports. The model is always the same. The strategist must scan the environment and look for favorable trends that can be exploited by specific strategies.

Opportunities in the finance industry

In the modern finance industry, we can see the search for opportunity at its core. Thousands of analysts (or so-called strategists) try to identify opportunities ahead of their competition. These opportunities may be economic, technological or social. An example of an economic opportunity is the decision of the US Federal Reserve in fall 2010[26] to start a new round of quantitative easing, where the central bank bought government securities (Treasuries) for generating liquidity in the market. That opened an opportunity to invest in gold and silver as prices went up. On April 31, 2011 Vanguard Precious Metals and Mining,[27] a mutual fund, posted an annualized return of 33.33 percent.[28] In regard to holding gold bullion or coins, the World Gold Council reported that demand increased by 29 percent in 2012.[29]

Sometimes opportunities are related to a specific industry. In the spring of 2009, when the US car industry was at its very bottom, long-term visionary analysts believed that car sales would pick up in 2010/2011[30] and recommended that their customers take advantage of very low stock prices of carmakers. Similar observations could be made about regions such as Asia after the crash of 1998, which was followed by the big boom of the 2000s, or single countries, as when Germany became very competitive in 2009 after the Euro devalued due to the crisis in Greece and Ireland.

Analysts and strategists work to identify opportunities in the form of potentially undervalued assets, whether they are entire economies, regions, industries, or individual companies. Analysts also look for overvalued assets that represent an opportunity for short selling.[31] The identified opportunities are recommended to customers of financial institutions (for example, stock rankings that range from "strong buy" to "sell").

Why does the modern investment industry have thousands of analysts and strategists to identify investment opportunities? A main reason is the industry's business model. To earn their fees, most brokers and banks advise their customers on investment options based on extensive research. To provide this service efficiently, the industry concentrates on standardized research. A competent advisor takes risk tolerance into consideration when discussing investment opportunities with his or her client, with the objective of generating maximum risk-adjusted returns.

Pitfalls of the finance industry

The investment industry primarily creates generic investment recommendations based on an analysis of opportunities without taking into account client skills and unique abilities. Investors receive and pay for advice that doesn't take into account their personal knowledge or competences.

The finance industry tends to focus on the short-term – one-to-two years. For true wealth building at least five or more years are necessary, not only because short-term fluctuations should be omitted from a strategic perspective but also because building personal competences can take years. Therefore the finance industry's work in opportunity analysis has only limited value for wealth building, as proven by returns in the stock and bond markets.

The strategic investor must analyze opportunities, by him or herself, and develop a clear concept on which to build a strategy. This cannot be done by casually reading the financial press or other financial publications since the investor has to build competences and identify real, attractive opportunities and trends.

Types of opportunities

From an investment perspective, any asset or asset class with growth potential (for returns) can represent an opportunity. This is a broad definition of an opportunity, but the investor needs to identify more specific opportunities. To illustrate, we draw on one of our interviews with Uwe, head of a family investment office, who told us the following story:

> In the mid-2000's we began to systematically look for attractive investment opportunities. It soon became obvious – and many

investment gurus such as Jim Rogers and Marc Faber agreed – that raw materials might be attractive. But which ones? We analyzed the big users of raw materials, including the car industry, talking to experts to find out which materials would be highly utilized by the car industry of the future. We discovered that rare earth metals would be on high demand and decided to concentrate our strategy on these materials.

Since the investor must build competences in a specific field, Uwe focused on a relatively small one. His specific knowledge enabled him to exploit that opportunity to create wealth. Had he been satisfied with a broad definition, such as "commodities," he would have found it much more difficult to build a successful strategy.

Finding opportunities: chance or methodology?

Successful investors often chance upon opportunities, as did Christian, who decided to buy his first classic Jaguar without looking for a specific model. His first classic might have been a Mercedes, a Ford Thunderbird or another brand, which did not appreciate as much in value, and it was by luck that Jaguars happened to appreciate quite nicely. But had Christian carefully evaluated all potential opportunities perhaps he would have chosen a Bugatti or a Ferrari which have done even better; one Bugatti sold for more than $30 million in 2012.[32]

Many opportunities, perhaps the majority, drop into our laps by accident, quite often from people we meet by accident or who approach us. But is this the right way? By choosing an opportunity we often define a path that has an immense impact on our lives. For example, the medical doctor's first investment in Georgia was the basis for many journeys to Georgia that established a long-term, close relationship to the country and its people.

Such "accidental" decisions can be considered lucky. It is advisable not to leave the identification of opportunities to chance. It is worth doing systematic thinking by applying an appropriate methodology.

Imagine if Christian's first classic car had been a 1950s Chevrolet
Corvette, not prized at auction and not ranked in the top classic
cars.[33] On the other hand, if his first purchase had been a Bugatti, his
investment would have done much better.

Start with your strengths

In June 2012, when many investors were panicking in the middle of
the Euro crisis and deteriorating economy, Jim Rogers, a well-known
commodity investing guru, said in an interview with Bloomberg:
"There are always opportunities; there are always people that build a
fortune even in these bad conditions."[34]

Even in difficult times, an investor planning a strategy may end
up with dozens or even hundreds of opportunities. It is essential to
consider the investor's strengths in this search process. According to
the 10,000 hours rule of Malcolm Gladwell, building strengths is very
time consuming and it is more efficient to exploit opportunities that
make use of existing ones. If there were enough opportunities that
meet the investor's strengths then there would be no need to continue
searching. But in many cases such a limited search leads to unsatisfactory results, and it becomes necessary to search further.

Do your homework: scan the environment

In the literature on strategic management, many authors recommend a
systematic information analysis as a first step,[35] including researching
the general environment, overall economic, technological and social
trends, and specific markets. A more detailed checklist for a general
information analysis can be found in the Appendix.

An analysis of opportunities should be performed not only as a
first step but also at regular intervals (for instance annually) to vali-
date earlier assumptions.

Apply a long-term view

If we start with the notion that most fields of investment go through a
more or less distinctive life cycle, it becomes crucial, from a strategic

perspective, to look for opportunities at the beginning of a long-term life cycle since it may take years for an investor to become a real master in a field.

Let's take the case of one of our co-authors who had a strength in technology innovation. After completing a PhD in applied physics at Cornell University, he was responsible for over ten years for the development of advanced technologies in the biomedical division of NASA-Johnson Space Center, where a number of his technologies were flown on the space shuttle program. In searching for opportunities where he could deploy his strength in technology innovation to make sound long-term investments, he identified a long-term life cycle in the healthcare sector and developed a focused investment strategy to take advantage of it. Recognizing a long-term need for efficiency gains within healthcare, he developed a specialized approach to identifying attractive investment opportunities in proven medical innovations that significantly improve patient outcomes while reducing total cost. This combination of an expertise in technology innovation and in investments led to a unique, differentiated strategy in the long-term cycle of the healthcare sector resulting in exceptional financial performance.

In another example, the concept of life cycles was applied by the Pühringer Gruppe, a highly successful family office, asset manager, and foundation in Austria and Switzerland. Pühringer aims to identify important life cycles in areas such as interest and quantitative easing, as well as in geographic regions. By applying this concept, the Pühringer ZZ1 Fund achieved an annual return of 20.88 percent, with a volatility of 19.34 percent, over the ten years 2003–2012, substantially higher than returns from the comparable Harvard Endowment Fund or the Yale Endowment Fund.[36]

Pitfalls of opportunities

What if the expected growth potential does not materialize or a crash occurs? This happened to investors who saw great potential in solar

Figure 5.2   Phoenix stock price

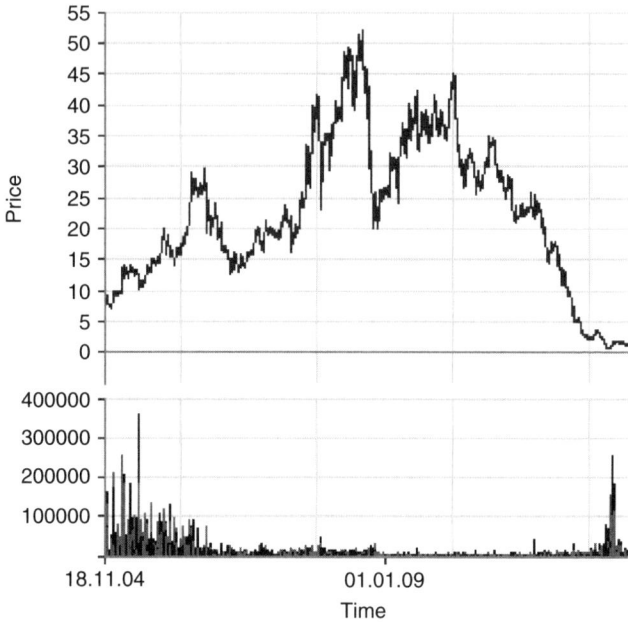

Source: Phoenix Solar Chart – Max – FSE, http://www.finanzen.ch/aktien/Phoenix_
Solar-Aktie?rd=fn

panels in the mid-2000s when this field was promising exceptional
investment returns given a growing awareness of environmental problems and a strong shift to alternative energy sources. In some countries,
such as Germany, the installation of solar panels was heavily subsidized
and many investors felt that the solar panel industry offered a major
opportunity at the beginning of a long-lasting life cycle.

During the mid-2000s these investors were proven right as companies that produced solar panels appreciated strongly. For instance, the
stock of Phoenix Solar AG, a German photovoltaic company, listed at
EUR 6.463 in 2004 increased to EUR 52.69 in 2008 (by 715 percent
since being listed). But, a few years later demand for solar power fell

and there was a collapse in stock prices. In May 2013 the Phoenix Solar stock price was down to EUR 1.43.[37]

If an investor had decided to invest in the solar panel industry in early 2000, even building a strong core competence in the field, he would not only have suffered significant financial losses after the crash, but his competences would be of little further use. This demonstrates that choosing an opportunity for strategic investing is no easy task. The opportunity must have a long-range positive potential and the investor must be aware of the risks that increase with the narrowness of the field of investment.

NETWORKS: SUPPORT OF WEALTH CREATION

In all strategic teachings, network strategies play a central role. In his book, *The Art of War*, Sun Tzu proclaims: "Assuming the proper intelligence network is in place, information will rapidly become available that illuminates how the enemy is reacting, where attacks have been successful and when forward progress has been stymied"[38] (McNeilly, 2001, p. 195). Genghis Khan, the founder of the Mongol Empire, was fully aware of this when he established strong networks with vassal princes who provided information vital to his conquests.[39] Similarly, in corporate strategy, networks and alliances, coalitions and joint ventures play a central role.[40]

Internet-based social networks such as Twitter and Facebook have ushered in a new era of networking as technology enables users to use networks in a highly efficient way. But the ease of social networking also results in disillusionment with network quality. The strategist must make sure that the networks relied on do in fact contribute to the success of the strategy.

Networks in finance

Networks have a long history in finance, starting with the Medici, a prominent Florentine family, bankers, politicians and clergy, most influential in the Renaissance. The Fuggers in Augsburg, powerful financiers who owned 10 percent of the Habsburg Empire's assets in the sixteenth century, like the Medicis, built and used extensive networks that reached across continental Europe. The Fuggers' international network allowed them to provide another critical service to the fragmented Habsburgs empire. As the vassal states paid money to the Habsburgs, the Fuggers were able to facilitate payments in multiple European currencies.[41]

Similar observations can be made of the Rothschilds, whose network of contacts enabled them to move money around Europe, even during wartime. A famous example, but only one of many, is Nathan's transfer of large sums of money from London to Portugal to pay the British troops in the Peninsular War.[42]

The Rothschild network ensured they were the first to learn about Wellington's victory at Waterloo, allowing them to make outstanding profits on the London stock exchange. Almost all financial market participants today try to make use of networks. Again and again the importance of networks to a successful investment strategy was emphasized in our interviews, as in the following examples.

Uwe Feuersenger, CEO of Aeris Capital (the family office of one of SAP's founders), and President of the Family Office Circle Foundation (FOCF), provides an excellent example of use of networks. His foundation consists of about 120 of the biggest family offices worldwide and allows members to exchange investment ideas, and discuss due diligence and risk management strategies.

Another good example of valuable networks in finance is the Internet platform created by one of the FOCF early members – the serial Internet entrepreneur Joachim Schoss – that allows collecting information from the best global providers to answer members' questions. The platform also gathers feedback and judgment from peers. Knowledge, experience and peer networking all have the potential to improve the strategic investment management process.

Why are networks so important?

The investment ecosystem is extremely complex, with millions of active investors influenced by microeconomic, macroeconomic, political, technological, social, and psychological factors. To make things even more complicated, investors regularly receive invitations, sales calls, and sales documentation from financial institutions selling their products. While it is practically impossible for an individual investor to track all these parameters, partners in the network can help in screening important trends and developments, and in assessing opportunities.

What kind of information can an investor obtain from his network? From a strategic perspective, specific information that helps to apply the strategic principles is essential in the implementation of the investment strategy. On the Internet and in other mass media, all types of public information are available to everybody almost immediately, so it becomes more and more difficult to find information that gives the investor an edge.

A network can provide private information on investment opportunities, for instance, companies to invest in, and other matters that can lead to strategic advantage. Valuable information can also be more general and concern new industries at the beginning of their life cycles. For example, in an investment club that meets every quarter each participant is expected to present one investment idea. In the early 2000s one investor strongly promoted investments in gold. After extensive discussions, many participants concluded that precious metals might be attractive and they invested in this asset class, which proved to be a wise investment decision at the time.

Information on threats and risks is especially valuable. For example, an investor may learn that a company he is investing in might be on the way to running into difficulties, which would enable him to divest in good times. This kind of information can support the investor's decision-making, saving time and lowering investment risk.

These elements are related to timing and a quality network can help an investor make the right decision at the right time.

Finally, there is the element of efficiency, and a network can show investors how to realize investments at lower cost.

Guidelines for building networks

The heart of the network: core competences

In the practical investment world, an investor has many possibilities for building networks: bankers and brokers, friends from clubs (Rotary, Lions, and so on), or other associations. The investor must always bear in mind that strengthening strategic core competences is the number one objective for setting networking priorities. Can the network provide the right information for strategic success by matching the investor's strategy? Answering the following questions might be useful:

- Which people or circles may be useful for the core competences I intend to build?
- Who are the gatekeepers for information about my core competences?
- Are there other people interested in the same field of investment?
- What seminars, conferences, or other events are attended by these people?

Of course, network development becomes a central issue after the strategist has defined his main field of investment. The investor must think about the network he must establish to implement the strategy. In the case of our co-author who had a successful career in the biomedical division of NASA, his analysis of the global trends in healthcare markets led him to focus on investments in health technology innovation. Having completed his MBA in finance, he analyzed the investment horizon for health technologies in the US and concluded that increasing regulatory barriers would cause significant delays in market access for medical innovation, making it more risky for investors in this sector. In his research he also learned that Europe had traditionally been very efficient in the introduction of medical innovation and that Switzerland had invested heavily in strengthening this sector. But how could he develop a network in Europe to gain knowledge of, and access to, promising investment opportunities?

Having chosen direct investments in proven medical innovation as his core focus strategy, in 2008 he decided to work with a non-profit organization in Geneva to launch the European Tech Tour MedTech Summit in Switzerland (today called European HealthTech Summit), an international competition in medical technology that brings together leaders in the industry to evaluate hundreds of companies and identify those likely to have a global impact in the healthcare sector. Leveraging the cumulative intelligence of this network, the Summit provides unique insights into market trends, with new senior executives coming from the industry into the network on a regular basis. Serving on the leadership team of the Summit as president, and subsequently chairman, enabled our co-author to build a strong network in the sector.

Networks are a two-way street

The final objective of networking is generating information for the investor. However, if the investor only seeks information from network partners without contributing, the partners will soon realize that the connection does not give them much in return and the network becomes less effective. A valuable network will only function if members are willing to contribute useful and interesting information.

Brian Uzzi, a globally recognized professor at the Kellogg School of Management, and Shannon Dunlap stress the "shared activities principle." Powerful networks are forged through high-stakes activities that connect (the investor) with others. Network activities should evoke a passion in participants: "These shared activities also forge ties between diverse individuals by changing their usual patterns of inter-action, letting them break out of their prescribed business roles"[43] (Uzzi and Dunlap, 2005, pp. 3–5).

The Forum for Innovative Finance, for example, a network of innovative entrepreneurs in the Swiss finance industry, was founded by one of our authors. Every quarter the members meet for a discus-sion of new trends in investing and investment opportunities. Each participant is obliged to make a specific contribution, such as presenting research results, practical experiences or specific invest-ment proposals. With active participation required, the events are well attended and experts ask to be invited on a regular basis.

Strong and weak ties

It is always dangerous if an investor starts to build a network with close friends or family. Uzzi and Dunlap call this the "self-similarity principle," which states that, when you make network contacts, you tend to choose people who resemble you in terms of experience, training, and worldview.

Close contacts often have the same information as the investor, but a network needs to provide new information to be valuable. Mark Granovetter, a professor of sociology at Stanford University, is best known for his 1973 work "The strength of weak ties" and labeling the most valuable contacts in a network as "weak ties"[44] because they are contacts with people who do not belong to one's close network. They may be new or casual contacts. Because weak tie contacts live in a different space, they can offer new information and insights to influence and improve your strategy.

One of our co-authors, for example, wanted access to the most sophisticated angel investors in his region to help improve his approach to investing. The co-author's close contacts (strong ties) were not able to provide useful information, and it was only after exploiting weak ties that a valuable new network could be established.

He began a publication project on angel investing, interviewing experts, and asking all his contacts to recommend other experts in the field. With time he was able to build a *Who's Who* of angel investors and, to improve collaboration within this network, he co-founded an informal association that gave him outstanding information on investing in early stage ventures.

To summarize, in planning network activities the investor should follow Granovetter's law and intentionally seek network partners who do not belong to his or her close circle and are more distant "weak ties."

Building your network strategy

To maximize quality of information, networks should be built in a systematic way. Let's consider again the case of Martin, who decided to concentrate on direct investments and build core competences in this field. An important element of his strategy was building a new specialized network to support his investments in different ways:

- Although Martin did not know about the findings of Granovetter, he intuitively realized that he had to establish new contacts, and he began to attend symposia, seminars, and workshops where he could meet new people active in direct investments. He not only relied on his existing contacts, but systematically built new contacts to develop new ties.
- Martin reactivated contact with his former employer and, with advice from this highly experienced investor, he learned about the risks associated with direct investments and structuring transactions, and he developed new ideas on helping the companies he invested in.
- He created alliances by joining a group of independent investors and consultants.
- For access to deal flow, he contacted M&A advisors, lawyers, and auditors.

- To contribute to his networks and create the necessary capacity to maintain them, he met with his network partners on a regular basis, sharing his own experiences.

DIFFERENTIATION: THE PATH TO UNIQUENESS AND COMPETITIVE ADVANTAGE

A central message of this book is that – especially in our times of deleveraging and low interest rates – sticking to traditional investment concepts will not create wealth. To build a fortune an investor must apply a different approach. The concept of differentiation must be inherent in the wealth-building process and strategic investing means doing something different from traditional investment approaches.

With millions of participants and intense competition differentiation becomes key to competitive advantage. We see this at work in the corporate ecosystem, where market differentiation plays a central role in strategy. Michael Porter, one of the leading authorities in corporate strategy at Harvard Business School, cautions: "A company can outperform rivals only if it can establish a difference that it can preserve"[45] (Porter, 1996, pp. 10–12). Robert Grant writes about differentiation advantage, quoting Robert Goizueta, former Chairman of Coca-Cola Company:

> If the three keys to selling real estate are location, location, location, then the three keys of selling consumer products are differentiation, differentiation, and differentiation.[46] (Grant, 2010, p. 245)

And John Templeton, one of the most influential investors of all time, is known for saying "If you want to have a better performance than the crowd, you must do things differently from the crowd"[47] (Templeton, 2012).

Successful differentiation: William's story

William, an employee of a small UK bank in the 1980s who was responsible for his clients' investments, made a puzzling observation that the efficient market theory described in the literature, and followed by many market participants, was not really working. According to the efficient market theory, all information relevant to the price formation of shares is reflected in the share quotations before an investor can use it (with the exception of insider information). Therefore, it is considered impossible to systematically outperform the market by using public investment information. However, he observed (as did a few others) that the financial market is a meeting point of different emotions and different reactions to the same information. He therefore began to investigate concepts of "behavioral finance."[48]

Behavioral finance suggests that emotions reflected in stock exchange language, such as greed and fear, belong to stable human behaviors and change little over time. Emotions get converted into actions and the actions of stock exchange participants form traces in the share price and volume progression. If emotions are relatively stable, one can assume that the developing traces are likewise stable and can be evaluated (measured). The stock market is an immense data universe from which the patterns formed by the emotional acts of the market participants can be discerned and converted into statistically and/or quantitatively evaluated algorithms.

By studying the literature, analyzing historical market information on price and volume, and conducting historical testing, William identified a series of usable short-term patterns in the market, based mainly on a short-term reversal to the mean. He went on to exploit the patterns and was able to systematically outperform the market. The probability of the patterns, enhanced by a set of filters, ensures that trades are initiated only in the direction of the longer-term trend of a certain stock. The money management rules follow common sense, such as: each trade shall not exceed 5 percent of the portfolio value; only invest in equities, and only in US markets (to gain the advantage of relatively larger volumes); only pool Russell 1000 stocks, and only stocks with a minimum turnover of USD 20 million per day. A set of exit rules completes the system.

The system is based on observable market inefficiencies obeying certain laws of probability and contradicting mainstream theory and practice. So long as this trading system remains proprietary (and used only for William's and his family's assets) it maintains its differentiation. If a system such as the one described here were published, in the near future it would no longer work because it would be traded by too many investors with large positions, and the exploitation of the patterns on which the system is built would become unproductive. In other words, the system's differentiation would be lost.

William differentiated by developing a system in a field where he had little competition. He applied rules ignored or neglected by the mainstream. Because he was not trading large sums compared to institutional traders, almost nobody was aware of his activities. In the terminology of strategy he applied the concept of the "indirect approach" perfectly. Over the last few years (including 2008 and 2009) the system often lost significant money (30 percent loss), but each time the strategy prevailed and he regained his investment. All and all he never had a negative year (although there have been negative quarters).

I have to buy two stocks every day, whether I think the market is going up or down, whether there is a revolution, whether the Euro cracks ... it does not matter. I have to buy my stocks and sell my stocks as dictated by my rules. Whether the market goes to 0 or to infinity, I have to buy and sell my stocks when the profit target or the holding period is reached, even if I expect the market to go up 10 percent. All emotions are cut off.

William systematically developed the core competences necessary for successful development and improvement of the model. It took him 10 years to develop, based on hours and hours of studying and reading. The work paid off with an investment strategy that differentiated him from other investors.

Prerequisites for successful differentiation

The investor must select a field for differentiation. William concentrated on small cap stocks, but his main concept for differentiation was his proprietary investment model. The field of investment can be chosen based on several considerations:

- Niche asset class such as early stage venture capital. William concentrated on small cap stocks. Warren Buffett concentrates on larger value stocks.
- Selection by industry. For instance, Dominique selected unquoted medical technology companies.
- Geography. Uli concentrated on China, and Martin selected the eastern part of Switzerland for his direct investments.

There are numerous possibilities for choosing a field of investment. William developed a proprietary mathematical investment model that differentiated him from the competition. This example highlights the utility of a combination of several fields in defining a real niche (in this case mathematical modeling and small cap stock investing). It also demonstrates how a narrow niche can be exploited successfully.

Building core competences for differentiation

Differentiation is no easy task because one must develop core competences. As we saw, it was only after extensive study and much trial and error that William achieved a model that generated profits.

Apply an indirect approach

The concept of the indirect approach plays a central role in military strategy. Leading writers such as Jomini[49] and Hart have stressed its importance. Hart explains, "With deepening reflection…I began to realize that the indirect approach had a much wider application – that it was a law of life in all spheres: a truth of philosophy"[50] (Hart, 1941, pp. 2–4).

At the heart of the concept of the "indirect approach" is the notion that a frontal attack is inefficient and leads to higher risk than a more camouflaged indirect one. By using an indirect approach the strategist keeps his intentions secret as long as possible. William used this concept well and, when asked by a friend about the algorithms of his investment model, said: "If two people make use of the same algorithm the profits are halved. Therefore I cannot give you any details." A general principle of the indirect approach is to not reveal the intentions of the investor and to be secretive. Thus the path of differentiation can be protected as long as possible.[51]

Be innovative

To apply his investment concept, William had to develop a completely new model. But there are many ways to innovate, often including a combination of different strategic principles.

Christian and Florence, for example, developed an innovative approach to real estate investment. Christian had a degree in finance and had worked at various institutions in operational management. His wife Florence was a physician and spent most of her time in her practice and at the hospital caring for her patients. Given the income they generated the couple enjoyed a comfortable lifestyle in Geneva, Switzerland, but with the birth of their first son their outlook on life changed, and they decided to focus on building a small fortune that could help secure their son's future.

Given their busy professional lives the couple decided to focus on their local surroundings for investment opportunities. Christian noticed that property prices in Geneva had been rising steadily while Florence, who always had a passion for modern design and decoration, often commented on the high quality of new construction. Christian spent a lot of time reading articles and talking to real estate professionals to understand housing valuations. By talking with his father-in-law, who had experience in the construction industry, he also learned about the challenges of renovation projects and some best practice approaches in managing them.

In brainstorming on their options the couple decided to focus on combining investments in real estate with refurbishing acquired flats and thus apply, in comparison to other investors in their surroundings, a differentiated investment approach. There were other refurbishing companies in the Geneva region and the couple had to find additional ways to differentiate. They used the strong credit rating of the family to obtain a significant fixed rate loan, and got advice on finding a suitable property from a good friend who was an agent in the housing market. Another element of differentiation was to buy material and appliances at low prices in neighboring France. In summary, the couple was able to generate 100 percent cash on cash in a little over two years, an excellent outcome of their investment strategy.

THREATS AND RISKS: PREVENTING LOSSES

An old rule in investing is that it is more important to prevent losses than to achieve gains,[52] because it usually takes a long time to make up for a loss. If an investor loses 50 percent of his wealth, what sort of gain does it take for him to return to square one? Not 50 percent, but a 100 percent gain to make up for the loss. The investor who wants to build wealth must undertake all measures to prevent losses, which stem from threats and risks. While threats are related to events that are not quantifiable, risks are related to events on which at least some information about the probability distribution is available. Martin, for example, confronted several threats in connection with his direct investments in unquoted companies, including the emergence of new competitors in the market of his portfolio companies, the introduction of new products, the loss of important employees, and dramatic currency fluctuations. He had no way of statistically quantifying these threats prior to his investment decision.

Another threat to Martin's investment portfolio was related to the non-quantifiable fat tail events that could impact his public market investments, such as the collapse of 2008. Martin's investments in the stock market were also exposed to some statistically quantifiable risks, where calculations about the probability of expected returns could be made using historical data.

Continuous wealth creation without setbacks is not possible

Almost every investor we interviewed experienced losses due to unexpected threats and risks. The investor who intends to build wealth cannot expect a continuous positive fortune-building process. Losses inevitably occur and must be anticipated.

For example, Paul Allen, co-founder of Microsoft, made a fortune and became one of the richest men in the US. After leaving the company he started making his own investments in IT, space technology, and sports. One of his worst investments was in cable TV, which turned out to be a bottomless pit. Again and again Allen had to pump additional cash into Charter, his chosen company. All these investments were made in vain and the company filed for bankruptcy in 2009 resulting in more than US$ 7 billion loss to Allen's wealth.[53]

John Maynard Keynes was well known as a successful investor, but in 1920 he lost his fortune and had to start from scratch. "Keynes learned a valuable but painful lesson – markets can act perversely in the short-term. Of this, he later famously commented: 'The market can stay irrational longer than you can stay solvent'"[54] (Harrod, 1990).

The same goes for many once famous hedge fund managers, including John Meriwether of LTCM,[55] Victor Niederhoffer,[56] and Nicholas Maounis Amaranth,[57] all of whom lost incredible amounts of money.

Throughout history wealth has been destroyed by events that include wars, be they wars of conquest, such as the Napoleonic wars or World War II, be they religious wars like the Thirty Years War in the seventeenth century where Protestants fought against Catholics, or civil wars like the Spanish Civil War. Similarly, there are many examples where riots, rebellions, and other violent events have destroyed considerable wealth.

Finally, wealth has been destroyed by pandemics, such as the Black Death, which originated in the fourteenth century in China, where majority of the population was killed, leaving a completely impoverished country (for more detail see Amy Chua's: *Day of Empire*[58]). In total, the plague drastically reduced the world population, killing an estimated 30 to 60 percent of Europe's population alone.

Because threats and risks can easily destroy all wealth, an investor's critical task is to think about what measures can prevent substantial setbacks.

How to deal with threats and risks

Are there guidelines the strategic investor can apply during the wealth creation process? We believe that the idea of pure quantification, as proposed by capital market theory, is of little value in the framework of strategic investment, and that more appropriate rules must be applied.

Rigorous analysis

What are the fundamental threats and risks that can substantially impede wealth creation? Managing threats and risks requires careful analysis of all potential events that can harm investments, and clear priorities have to be established. The establishment of such a list requires a thorough understanding of the investments, and here again we see the importance of focus investments.

Uli concentrated his investments on China and Asia and, because he already had a broad knowledge of the region and its markets (a core competence), he was in a good position to identify potential threats and risks. But the strong focus on these regions also gave him an information advantage with regard to unexpected events. He was able to learn about unexpected regional events as they occurred and was able to react with short notice.

We asked Dominique, an investor in medical technology, about his views on risks and how he controls them:

People often think that technology is the biggest risk, but I disagree. Technology risk is mostly visible, you see it coming. People are the biggest risk (ourselves and those we hire). Also, you can make a mistake by missing information on the market, or on the competition. This is the second biggest risk – i.e., missing something very crucial. I mitigate this type of risk by keeping to a limited number of investments.

Competent investors know that investing requires courage and the ability to take risks. But they also know that there is only a small difference between courage and foolishness. Courage means that the investor collects all possible information, analyzes it, and takes all factors into consideration before making an investment decision. Foolishness on the other hand means making investment decisions without due consideration of all pertinent information. But, in a highly complex world where one is often unable to know all the facts, only time may prove whether a decision was courageous or foolish.

Investment decisions are uncertain to a degree and, because unpredictable "black swan" events can occur at any time, experienced investors know that, as a fallback position, part of the wealth should be invested in highly secure assets such as cash and secure bonds. The objective here is wealth protection and not wealth creation. These security investments may, to some extent, also incorporate different asset classes, and diversify with different stocks or a hedge fund of funds.

Nassim Taleb underscores this necessity by showing that, based on systems stability, many small, uncorrelated subunits can best contribute to this objective.[59] Given the high risk associated with unexpected power law, or "black swan," events, the investor should build a security portfolio whose sole objective is to ensure survival in a worst case scenario. An investor has to expect and survive these kinds of rare events, and allocation to the security portfolio is a crucial mitigation strategy to manage unpredictable threats.

Careful selection of the core competences to be built

Strengths and core competences must also incorporate the management of threats and risks. Threats are the opposite of opportunities but are clearly related to them. Significant opportunities usually come with considerable threats and risks. Think of an investor in the early 2000s when investment in US real estate seemed to be very attractive. Many investors chose this asset class and tried to build core competences in it. When the US real estate market collapsed in 2008, know-how in that market became more or less obsolete.

In defining what core competencies to build, an investor must consider the cyclical nature of the asset class and the potential creation and bursting of bubbles within the sector. Through historical analysis and careful consideration of the environmental factors, an informed investor will have a better chance of predicting cycles and avoiding the devastating effects of bubbles bursting.

Building core competences has far-reaching consequences. Too many people decide on their core competences intuitively, without thinking about associated threats and risks, relying instead on general opinion and what others are doing. They may be lucky for a while, but this is not the way to create sustained wealth. The thoughtful investor will analyze the options from the point of view not only of opportunities but also of associated threats and risks.

Risk management by concentration of forces

In modern finance, diversification is at the center of risk management since finance applies mathematical tools for this purpose with no room for qualitative, motivational, or organizational considerations. But these factors may have a detrimental impact on risk control and investment success.

Ralf Biggadike, a professor at Columbia University, analyzed a number of company diversification projects and found that small diversification projects received little attention, because senior managers thought that if they failed with a project, they still had enough other potentially successful projects.[60] But when confronted with larger projects, senior managers reasoned that, with much at stake, they should concentrate all efforts (such as motivational and organizational) on the project to ensure success. Biggadike's findings indicate that when managers concentrate forces in this manner the risk of failure decreases.

Similarly, when it comes to constructing investment portfolios, investors should concentrate their investments in a focus portfolio (described later in Chapter 7) to reduce risk by carefully monitoring the portfolio and, if necessary, taking appropriate action.

Christian and Florence, for example, concentrated on investing in and refurbishing condominiums only in the Geneva region. Focusing on one small field of investment enabled them to monitor their investments closely. Christian calculated the risk and potential return on a weekly basis by keeping a careful watch on the local real estate market, as well as carefully managing the financial risk through budget control on each project. His focus portfolio enabled him to stay close to his investments and keep track of potential risks. This approach helped him prevent unanticipated losses, thereby improving the performance of his investments.

An investor must track developments in his focus investments and become an expert in the field. By concentrating efforts, the investor can improve his strengths and competences as he gains more experience and increases his expertise. By staying alert to unexpected developments, the investor can detect risks and threats early and thus implement counter measures at the earliest possibility.

Avoiding threats and risks

An investor can often avoid a specific threat or risk. If an investor in 2007 had invested in US real estate but anticipated a bubble that might burst not too far in the future, he or she could have evaded this threat by choosing another asset class, or by keeping funds in cash.

In another example, if an investor continues to put money in so-called "risk free" assets, such as US Treasuries, there is still no such thing as a risk free asset and threats and risks are associated even with this type of investment. One risk is the prospect of high inflation. After Quantitative Easing I, II, III, and IV, a tremendous amount of money was created that could lead to inflation. Even if inflation does not reach 1980 levels – more than 14.8 percent[61] – value destruction by inflation can be considerable.

Use of options and derivatives

One way to deal with threats and risks is the use of options and other derivative instruments that can reduce risk. Suppose in 2010 an investor, as part of his security portfolio, invested 2 percent of his net worth in physical silver. In 2010 and 2011 silver performed very well, the price rising from US$ 25 an ounce to close to US$ 49.82 on April 25, 2011.[62] Given the sharp rise in the price of silver this investor might suspect a bubble forming in the market for silver. He has the option of selling all or part of his silver to limit his exposure to the potential threat of a bubble burst. But because he holds the silver in physical ballots, selling would incur significant costs. Therefore, it would have been advisable to buy silver put options to protect against a drop in the price of silver.[63] This approach of "insuring" part of the portfolio provides a way to protect investments.

The use of futures and derivatives in risk mitigation is well known to hedge fund and other asset managers. For example, some asset management firms develop sophisticated factor models for investing in stocks, and to reduce volatility they reduce market exposure by taking short positions in related futures and ETFs,[64] especially important in case of unpredictable "black swans" or fat tail events.

Build networks

Another method for managing threats and risks is to build and use networks effectively. For example, one of our interview partners established a close relationship with a research firm which specializes in risk analysis of financial markets. Gaining access to such specialized risk analyses can provide valuable insights in support of risk control of investments.

Don't over-leverage

A final aspect of risk is leverage, which allows an investor to magnify returns through leveraging. Quite often the higher returns necessary for building wealth are only possible with leverage. But the more leverage an investor applies the more risk there is. Paul Allen, co-founder of Microsoft, who lost US$ 7 billion in his investment in the Charter Cable Company, said he considered the high leverage he took as a key cause of failure: "Most of all, I failed to understand the downside of over-leveraging. My dreams of a wired world empire finally sank under the weight of Charter's mountain of debt"[65] (Allen, 2011).

Leverage plays a central role in strategic investment management since it can either help wealth creation or destroy it. For example, Rolland-Yves, a pharmaceutical investor and one of our interview partners, believes in zero leverage: "No debt is a good way to manage risk! We own a lot of real estate, pharmaceutical assets, and positions in ten small companies with excellent intelligence, but we have no debt! We do not diversify in other asset classes except in real estate. We invest in other private companies in our sector that have an aligned philosophy and think for the long-term. Success for today is only visible the day after tomorrow!" Without leverage, Rolland-Yves has been able to maintain a long-term view on his investments without debt burdens and with little risk of default and restructuring.

We cannot define general rules for leverage since personal risk appetite and personal situations are fundamental to decisions on leverage. For instance, an investor in his or her late thirties can take more risk (and more leverage) in comparison to a 60-year-old. If a young investor fails, many active years remain to make a new start.

The older investor, however, does not have the luxury of time and must be more cautious.

A final word on threats and risks. Research on wealth creation is always biased because a researcher inevitably has to concentrate on successful investors. It is difficult to identify (and interview) unsuccessful ones. This sample bias omits the many investors who tried to build wealth but failed due to unexpected negative events, threats, and risks. We seldom learn about these failures, and to overcome this sample bias we try to identify and communicate causes of failure using real examples where detailed information is available. In our private interviews with successful investors we aimed to understand and communicate what worked for them in addressing threats and risks, and what failed, in order to provide a comprehensive view of strategic imperatives that increase chances of investment success.

Diversification

It is extremely difficult to forecast political and economic developments, which is why investors are urged to diversify. John Kenneth Galbraith, the Canadian-American economist, writes: "The only function of economic forecasting is to make astrology look respectable."[66]

The same goes for financial markets. Steve Davidson, a financial advisor with Wells Fargo Advisors, notes: "Forecasting future events is often like searching for a black cat in an unlit room, that may not even be there"[67] (Hitoshi and Claus, 2012, p. 85). If forecasting is not possible, diversification is the only way to offset losses in one investment with gains in others.

But applying the concepts of capital market theory – of which diversification is a cornerstone – leads to mediocre returns. By taking this road, it is almost impossible to create substantial wealth. The investor has a dilemma. Either he or she reduces risk by diversifying and concentrating on wealth preservation, or he or she achieves wealth creation by taking substantial risks and managing those risks by concentrating efforts to build outstanding competences for specific fields of investment.

Investors who have already built some wealth can use part of it as an additional instrument of risk management through diversification. But this can never be the field of real wealth creation because that can only happen when the investor develops outstanding competences in a narrow range of asset classes, regions, or fields of investment.

TIMING: LIMITED STRATEGIC CHOICES

Building core competences is always time consuming. In 2004 Jeremy decided, as did many American investors, to concentrate on real estate. He bought several well-located condominiums in Atlanta and, to become more professional, attended real estate seminars and collaborated with a friend with extensive experience in this field. He continued to improve his know-how and by 2008 became a specialized investor in condos in Atlanta. But 2008 was the year the US real estate bubble burst and he not only lost money on his investments, but also lost the value of his competences until the next positive real estate cycle, which could be years away.

This example clearly illustrates the importance of timing when the investor decides on which core competences to build. But there is also a short-term perspective of timing, when the investor must ask whether it is the right moment to make an investment or whether to wait.

Guidelines for successful timing: cycles

Most asset classes or fields of investment are subject to cycles. For instance, the long secular cycles at the stock exchange are well known; and the bull market cycles from 1949 to 1966 and from 1982 to 2000 are well documented. But between 1966 and 1982 we had a clear bear market cycle, and the period that began in 2001 and that may have ended in 2010 belongs in this category.[68] Investment cycles occur in other fields as well. For instance, the last commodity cycle (non-energy) went from 1975 to 2010 with declining (real) prices between 1975 and 2000 and rising prices between 2000 and 2010.[69] These cycles occur in other asset classes, such as real estate, regions (like the rise of China since 1990) and industries (such as information technology and telecom).

In general the upswing of a life cycle lasts from 10-to-30 years.

An investor's strategic planning for a wealth-building process usually begins when he or she is 35 to 45 years old. Therefore, an investor can at most decide twice in a lifetime which asset class or field of investment to concentrate strategic investments in and build the necessary core competences. If the investor gets the decision right there is a chance to build a fortune. If it is wrong, the opportunity is probably lost for a long time.

When is the best time to enter a life cycle of a field of investment? Too many investors make the decision too late, when the media are talking about the opportunity, as in the Internet bubble of the late 1990s. In 2000 many investors were prepared to pay any price for Internet stocks and smart businessmen were cashing in on so-called "concept IPOs," where only a business plan was presented to investors, most of whom got burned!

The investor should concentrate on the very early stage of a cycle. Often, it is more advantageous to start building core competences in the last stages of decline of a cycle, which means an investor can make the first investments at the bottom of the cycle when prices are lowest and competition is minimal. In 2013 this might have been the case for real estate in the US and certain European countries. Many brokers and investors went out of business and in many countries prices approached the bottom turning point of the cycle.

Timing is also an issue for operational investment decisions. There is a Wall Street saying: "Sell in May and go away!,"[70] referring to the fact that since World War II the performance of stocks from

May through October is relatively weak in comparison to the period November through April. This is certainly a simplistic rule but in the field of chart technique a whole science has been developed that should help the investor to time investments correctly.

Apply the big picture

In our day-to-day life we know how the stock exchange is doing from minute to minute. However, when an investor has to decide on a field of concentration, daily information is of no value. On the contrary, it even can be harmful because our brains heed the newest information more than the older, known as "recency effect."[71]

Understanding life cycles require a big picture approach. The investor must take a long-term perspective by analyzing developments over the previous 20-to-50 years. What were the life cycles in the past? How strong were they? Where do we stand today? How will the life cycle evolve in the future? In many cases, a thorough study of economic history, described in books such as *The Ascent of Money* by Niall Ferguson[72] or *This Time is Different* by Reinhart and Rogoff, may be useful.[73]

Clarify your investment horizon

A defining element of timing relates to the time horizon of the investment. Some investments, such as buying and refurbishing condominiums, will reach maturity within a relatively short time, while others, such as investing in drug development, may take a decade or longer.

Moreover, the stage in the life cycle of the field of investment must be considered when defining the investment horizon. By 2010 in the US real estate market, some specialists suggested that the inflection point indicating the end of price declines had been passed. In 2013 there were other professionals who believed it would still be quite some time before prices reached the lowest point. A strategic investor who plans to enter the real estate market must be aware of the uncertainty, and takes a long-term perspective, making it less important whether the turning point happens in 2012, 2013 or 2014.

Assure your strategic flexibility

The concentration of forces has a price – the risk of losses if the field does not develop as expected. Therefore, some flexibility to react should be built into the investment strategy. How can this be achieved?

One solution is to have financial reserves, as in the example of Martin who made sure that he always had reserves at his disposal. First it was his house and later he built a hedge fund portfolio unrelated to his main field of investment in non-quoted private companies.

The most challenging aspect of timing is flexibility since forecasts are difficult to make in finance. Events in financial markets do not unfold according to a normal distribution but are subject to power laws. The investor must ask whether to stick to the strategy and build core competences or whether to change strategic direction. There is no general rule that can be followed so the investor needs to make the decision according to his or her special situation.

Be creative and courageous

When World War II ended, Rudi was a 30-year-old clerk in a small Swiss town 10 miles from the German border. German industry was completely destroyed during the war, there was no transportation into Germany, and nobody wanted to buy German stocks so they were available at a bargain price. And because the banking system did not work, it was not possible to go to a Swiss bank and buy German stocks.

Since the cheap industrial German stocks represented a unique opportunity, Rudi took his father's handcart and all his savings and walked the 10 miles to the German border. After some discussion the French occupation forces allowed him to enter Germany, and he walked two additional miles to a bank in a small German border town where he bought all the available German industrial stock, including Höchst, Bayer, and Thyssen. He put the papers in his handcart, walked back to his home town, put the documents in the cellar and waited. By the end of the 1950s he was one of the town's wealthiest citizens.

What can we learn from this example? At the end of World War II the German stock cycle was at its lowest point. Nobody wanted to buy German stocks, which was also made difficult by the destroyed banking system. The success of Rudi's investment strategy was mainly due to two elements. First, he realized the tremendous opportunity inherent in German stocks at the end of the war. Although many other people saw this opportunity, very few had the courage to exploit it. Second, he developed a creative way to exploit the opportunity by taking his father's handcart and walking to Germany to buy the stocks.

This example shows that occasionally there are opportunities an investor can exploit even without building core competences. But in these cases the investor has to be courageous and creative. Courageous means willing to take big risks.

Be patient

Rudi was not out for short-term gain. He put the stock certificates in his cellar and waited, and it took more than 10 years for his strategy to pay off. A similar approach can be seen in the case of Bernard Arnault, the French billionaire businessman and chairman of LVMH, who said, "I think in business you have to learn to be patient. Maybe I'm not very patient myself. And I think what I've learnt the most is to be able to wait for something and get it when it's the right time"[74] (Arnault, 2005).

Strategic investing always has a long-term perspective. Therefore, the investor must be willing to apply a long-term perspective and be patient.[75]

EFFICIENCY: A PREREQUISITE FOR VALUE CREATION

Fees can hamper wealth creation

Every system or organization should use its resources in an efficient manner. Costs must be kept under control, otherwise the value created can be eaten up. In investment management this becomes particularly true. Transaction costs, brokerage fees, other banking fees, and taxes can easily make up more than 2 percent of the portfolio value. If the investor concentrates on special fields like direct investments, real estate investments or other specialty investments, this percentage is much higher. If we assume that the investor achieves a gross internal rate of return of 10 percent, costs can reduce this amount by a fifth or even a quarter. Compounded over several years, the loss can be substantial.

But efficiency is more than just watching and reducing fees and costs since they are generated throughout the whole strategic investment process. Investors must gather information on investment opportunities, threats, and risks efficiently. How can investor strengths and core competences be built at low cost? How can an investor use networks to reduce costs?

Another issue is the decision-making process, which can absorb resources and contradict the principle of efficiency. This was the case in a private equity company where the president was keen to keep risks to a minimum. Again and again he raised questions, asking his staff for additional information. The company missed several interesting opportunities and the costs associated with information gathering reduced the company's financial performance.

Smart investors with family offices also watch costs carefully. One of our interviewees with a family office of several hundred million dollars employs just one investment manager and one secretary. Because he designed a productive network, he can keep costs to a minimum.

Ongoing control of costs is a necessity for all investors, including costs for:

- Brokerage fees
- Fund management fees
- Taxes

- Consultancy fees
- Operating expenses of investment managers
- Administrative fees

As efficiency gains within the finance industry place competitive pricing pressures on providers, controlling and reducing costs will allow accessing better services at lower costs, especially on commoditized offerings.

Using networks effectively

Several of our interviewees indicated that effective use of networks can save money. For example, one interviewee, who inherited an insurance company and then sold it, started a Single Family Office with the proceeds. However, he did not enjoy the cost side of investing because the fee structures of many providers were not as transparent as he would have liked. To become more efficient he had to increase the size of assets managed, so he reached out to other families to manage their assets together with his to reduce management costs, increase bargaining power, and increase transparency.

Opportunity costs

Opportunity costs often receive less attention than they deserve. The term refers to the value an investor could have created if he had not pursued the chosen alternative. Let's assume an investor plans to invest $100,000 in stocks and initially considers two companies, A and B, but purchases shares in company A. After some time the value of company A stock increases by 10 percent to $110,000. But during the same period the stock of company B has gone up 50 percent, and his investment would have been worth $150,000. Thus the opportunity cost of the decision to buy shares in company A is $40,000.

In economics, opportunity costs are defined as the cost of any activity measured in terms of the value of the next best alternative foregone.[76] In investments, opportunity cost expresses the relationship between scarcity and choice and plays a crucial part in ensuring that an investor's scarce resources are used efficiently.

Chris, for example, was a management consultant who became a professional investor in the early 2000s. He already had a few successful investments, and was looking for other opportunities. In 2008 he was approached by a 40-year-old entrepreneur who had developed an innovative consulting product that could be used as a basis for strategic and operational planning. Chris was impressed by the product and, due to his extensive know-how of the consulting business, he was convinced that this product would be very successful and could be sold to other consulting companies worldwide. Several customers had already bought the product and a large auditing company was ready to sign a contract. In 2009 Chris took a 30 percent stake in the company and started to support the entrepreneur in sales presentations, seminars, and other activities. He invested over 25 percent of his time on these activities.

But by spring 2010, serious problems were emerging with many customers, who believed the product was useful but the software had too many bugs and support from the company was unsatisfactory. After talking to customers, Chris discussed the problems with the entrepreneur, who took his criticism personally, became angry, and asked his wealthy father to buy up Chris's shares. By the end of 2010 the transaction was closed. The sales price was 5 percent higher than the original price Chris had paid.

Looking at the transaction from the point of view of buying and selling stocks, it was not a big success but there was no failure because no loss occurred, even though in fall 2010 the company almost went bankrupt, and Chris could have lost his investment had he remained an investor in the company.

But if we look at this investment from the point of view of opportunity costs it looks completely different. Because Chris was fully absorbed with his new investment, he had no time to identify new investment opportunities. After 2008 Chris made only one investment, the company described above, and by 2011 he was sitting on a large cash position searching for new opportunities. He reflected:

> Originally I assumed that I could achieve an annual return of over 25 percent from my investment in the company. In the almost two years my money was invested I expected a return of over 50 percent. Because my sales price was only 5 percent higher than the original investment, I actually missed almost 45 percent in value creation. Looking back, I should have been more careful with the investment and concentrated on other investments offered to me during 2008 and 2009. I ended up with high opportunity costs.

He added:

> Looking back on 15 years as a private investor, the highest costs I ever generated were by far opportunity costs. I made several investments where I did not achieve the expected returns. In one case the company went bust and I had to invest a lot of time in legal suits. As an individual investor, my time to search for other investment opportunities, or even for supporting my successful investments, was limited. Every investor should consider personal time as the most critical resource and think of the opportunity costs of misallocating this resource.

What can be done to limit opportunity costs?

Information analysis can help. For example, an entrepreneur friend had known the founder of the company Chris invested in since childhood. Later Chris learned that this entrepreneur knew about the founder's problematic personality and would have been able to caution him, but he neglected contacting him for advice. In retrospect Chris would have benefited from better due diligence through his network on the personality of the founder.

Another way to limit opportunity costs is to apply an options approach that can hedge costs. Since the investor begins with only a small exposure, with the option to increase the investment in a given time based on specific milestones, he can monitor the development of the original investment to assess its opportunity cost. Because only a small amount is invested it is easy to stop the commitment of time and other resources and use them for other new investment activities if necessary.

The people dimension is a key factor in prevention of opportunity costs. In Chris's case the problem was not the consulting product, which was exceptional, but the entrepreneur, who was a poor manager unable to fulfill the promises he made to his customers. This is not an exception. Looking at our interviews and our own experiences, high opportunity costs are almost always related to human factors. If the people involved in investments had been checked carefully, it would have been possible to identify weaknesses and threats early on.

Be selective

Investors must be selective since, especially when they are successful, an endless line of people will approach from all sides with invest-ment ideas and opportunities. If the investor accepts proposals too quickly and invests even small amounts, he or she is spending time and opportunity cost by becoming involved. The longer this process lasts the more difficult it becomes to end the commitment, leading to increasing opportunity costs.

But the same thing can happen if the investor has too few opportu-nities at his or her disposal. Again the investor can choose an invest-ment too early and hamper efficiency. The goal is to optimize the number of opportunities. Too many investment opportunities may be a threat, but too few are also a problem. The investor must have sufficient opportunities available, and then be selective.

Three dimensions of efficiency

Achieving efficiency is an ongoing task when developing and imple-menting an investment strategy:

- First, efficiency means implementing a strategy to achieve low transaction costs and low banking fees (or low operational costs in general).

- Second, efficiency means applying the strategic principles described in the framework at low costs.
- Third, the savvy investor always bears in mind opportunity costs. Every strategic initiative has its costs and absorbs resources, especially the personal time of the investor which is then not available for other, perhaps more promising activities. When one investment fails, the related opportunity costs can be especially burdensome.

MAKING USE OF THE FRAMEWORK OF
STRATEGIC INVESTING

The principles of investing are interlinked. For instance, if we are looking for a niche for differentiation we have to explore the opportunities within this niche and determine whether we have strengths, or can develop strengths, for the niche. When we look at opportunities, we need to take into account related threats and risks. Thus, a first necessity in using the framework is applying a holistic view, not conducting isolated analyses of a single principle, but keeping the overall framework in mind.

Another issue is the sequence of analysis. While general rules cannot be applied to every situation, we can provide some guidelines. In our framework we placed strengths at the heart of the framework to document the fundamental importance of investor competences. Investors must analyze the strategic opportunities to be exploited in the focus portfolio from the perspective of strengths.

The primary question is, are there opportunities in fields where the investor has specific strengths? If possible, the investor should concentrate on exploiting strategic (investment) opportunities where he or she already possesses specific strength. If there is no match other opportunities should be considered.

Another issue is the information overload related to opportunities. Sources of information have to be ranked, which is where the network comes into play. Through networks we know our partners directly, allowing us to judge the competence and reliability of the source of information better than when we rely on anonymous information.

Another issue is the relationship between opportunities and threats. Outstanding opportunities often come hand in hand with considerable threats and risks and must be evaluated carefully.

With differentiation, the investor should not hunt opportunities where big crowds are active, and he should look for opportunities in small niches.

A further relationship exists with timing, especially when it comes to choosing the central opportunities at the core of the strategy. Opportunities are related to strong megatrends which, as we saw in the timing section above, are subject to life cycles. This means that good opportunities mostly exist at the beginning of a life cycle. Thus the time dimension, in the form of life cycles, must be carefully evaluated when making decisions on the central opportunities to be exploited.

Finally, identifying opportunities is always related to costs. As we heard over and over in our interviews, networks can be a useful tool to generate sound information at relatively low cost.

STRATEGIC ASSET ALLOCATION

Using the strategic investment framework, the investor should think of four different sub-portfolios.

First, to build wealth the investor has to select a field in which a considerable part of the funds will be invested. In this *Focus Portfolio* the investor shall leverage on specific strengths and core competences, and draw upon the networks he or she has built to achieve outstanding performance.

Investments are always exposed to threats and risks and the investor should allocate reserves to a *Security Portfolio* that can be used in case of power law or "black swan" events. These reserves should be placed in highly secure assets such as cash, secure AAA bonds, gold, or other precious metals.

In order to achieve diversification, part of the funds could be invested in assets with relatively high liquidity, such as stocks of well-established multinational companies. The advantage of investments in this *Diversification Portfolio* is that they provide a certain diversification to the focus investments while generating dividends or interest income.

Finally, in financial markets new opportunities often emerge, even though the investor may not have outstanding competences in the emerging field. We recommend building a (relatively small) *Opportunity Portfolio* in order to exploit extraordinary opportunities when they arise.

Thus, by using the strategic investment framework, the investor shall allocate assets to four distinct sub-portfolios:

- The Focus Portfolio: where the investor intends to achieve – due to his or her outstanding strengths and competences – outstanding investment returns and create true value.
- The Security Portfolio: which contains the reserves of last resort. The funds in this portfolio are invested in highly secure and liquid asset classes.
- The Diversification Portfolio: which constitutes a certain reserve as well as allowing the investor to diversify and reduce risk while generating some dividend and interest income.
- The Opportunity Portfolio: which allows for (rather small) investments to exploit special opportunities when they arise.

Every individual investor must define what percentage of his or her wealth should be invested in the four sub-portfolios. A young and aggressive investor can place a considerable amount into the focus or even the opportunity portfolio, whereas a conservative investor would rather promote large diversification, and make a relatively larger allocation to the security portfolio. Application of these four portfolios is further discussed in Part II.

Part II

HOW TO BE A SUCCESSFUL STRATEGIC INVESTOR

Chapter 6

TWO PATHS TO YOUR INVESTMENT STRATEGY

HOW PAUL BECAME A SUCCESSFUL INVESTOR BY CRAFTING HIS STRATEGY

After completing his education as an electrician and working for a few years in a large electrical installation company, Paul started his own business in a small European town some 30 years ago. At first there were only two employees – Paul and his wife – but Paul soon opened an outlet selling appliances and other products. Without the cash to buy the real estate, he rented the shop.

From the outset the company generated a good profit and, knowing the risks of being a self-employed entrepreneur, Paul and his wife placed any unspent money in their savings account, which soon amounted to the equivalent of several hundred thousand euros. Paul was regularly approached by his bank manager who proposed that he buy stocks rather than keep all his money in cash, but he always said: "I don't understand stocks, and therefore I prefer to have cash in my bank account."

In the late 1980s the building where Paul's shop was located was put up for sale and, since he had the cash, Paul decided to buy it.

Another building in the neighborhood soon came up for sale and since the price was quite reasonable Paul decided to buy that building as well. His investment strategy was emerging: to channel the cash flow that he generated from his electrical installation business into his savings account and use the money to invest in real estate. Over the years the value of his real estate investment grew to be greater than the value of his electrical installation business, and Paul became, first and foremost, a real estate investor.

From a strategic viewpoint, Paul obviously had a sharp investment strategy: invest surplus cash in real estate and refrain – with the exception of cash – from all other asset classes.

Paul's strategy was not the result of a formal process. In fact, he started with just one decision, to buy the building where his shop was located. Because this decision was successful, he made a second "strategic" decision by buying the next building, and because of that success he made additional investments in real estate. It only emerged over time that Paul was applying a clear strategy. Other elements of the strategy, such as always having an adequate amount of cash available, were the result of practical reasoning. Paul never wrote a strategy paper since his strategy was so simple that he could just keep it in his head.

Paul's story shows that a sound investment strategy can quite often emerge out of a first trial investment and repeating the investment in the same field several times. Many of our interviews confirmed that investor strategies often emerge through such a process. For instance, Christian bought the first Jaguar in his collection because he and his wife were keen to own a convertible sports car. It could have been another brand but they loved their Jaguar so much that a second Jaguar had to be bought. Only step by step did the acquisition of Jaguar sports cars become a deliberate investment strategy.

Henry Mintzberg, one of the best known strategy experts, calls the process by which a strategy slowly emerges through repetition of similar decisions, "crafting strategy." Mintzberg found this strategy implemented across many businesses and industries.[1]

HOW RALPH DESIGNED HIS INVESTMENT STRATEGY WITH A FORMAL PROCESS

In the 1980s Ralph was an assistant professor in mathematics who founded his own company specializing in banking software. In the late 1990s he sold his company for a good price and started to invest the proceeds. After gaining experience by listening to several bank brokers, Ralph decided to systematically develop his own investment strategy and conducted an extensive information analysis, asking questions that were particularly relevant from a strategic perspective.

First, he thought about the strengths he could build his strategy on. His outstanding know-how was in mathematics, a starting point. But, as a former entrepreneur, he also knew company management and thought he could use his mathematical know-how in hedge funds, and his management know-how in private companies.

He next thought about opportunities that were available to him. Ralph checked out several fields, and at this time (in the 1990s) hedge funds as an asset class were doing very well. Because these funds applied mathematical models, Ralph decided it would be an interesting asset class for him. He also considered private equity and venture capital funds because he had established a good network in those circles by selling his company. He knew he had to differentiate himself from other investors and hedge funds emerged as quite an attractive sector to focus on.

After additional research and analysis, Ralph developed some alternative strategies. His first strategy was to concentrate on private equity funds, where he had experience and a strong network. The second alternative was to concentrate on hedge funds where he could use his mathematical competences. And a third alternative was direct investments in non-quoted companies, which would allow him to use his know-how as a former entrepreneur.

Ralph was convinced there were good opportunities in all three fields. After evaluating the alternatives and creating a spreadsheet, he concluded that concentrating on hedge funds would fit his needs best. He put this new strategy on paper and began to implement it systematically.

This approach, where relevant information is analyzed, alternatives developed and, finally evaluated, is the method of "designing" strategy.[2] Having shown two primary ways to create a strategy we want to consider the advantages and disadvantages of each method.

CRAFTING VS. DESIGNING STRATEGY

The concept of "crafting strategy" certainly has its merits. The strategy just "emerges" over time as the investor makes a first decision (like buying a property), often intuitively, with gut feeling playing a significant role. Subsequent decisions about comparable additional investments are also made "intuitively."

An advantage of the crafting approach is that the practical testing of the strategy is built in, as in the case of Paul. His first investment in real estate was successful, which motivated him to make a second similar investment that also succeeded and then a third, and so on. He had the time to measure the outcome as each new investment was tested, and their success motivated Paul to make similar investments until a proven strategy emerged.

In the informal and often intuitive process of crafting strategy, personal preferences and interests play an central role. This subjective element ensures a strong emotional engagement to the strategy, involving excitement, passion, and devotion, resulting in a strong motivation that supports success by helping the investor concentrate on the preferred field and not deviate from the strategy.

Crafting a strategy has some critical disadvantages since the investor usually does not consider alternatives, and it is not clear whether there would have been other, more advantageous strategies. For instance, Christian just happened to buy a Jaguar as his first sports car and his strategy to invest in Jaguars evolved from this first decision. But was the concentration on Jaguars really the best solution? Today we know that Bugattis and Ferraris have appreciated more. But there were other completely different strategic investment options open to Christian. For instance, as a chemist he could have invested in start-up pharmaceutical companies.

Furthermore, because emotions and other subjective factors dominate the strategic focus, risks and threats may not be considered adequately enough. Many collectors learn this, and many real estate investors have a similar experience. During the boom years in the US, for example, real estate investors developed a passion for investing for short-term gain, but because strong emotions played a dominant role they paid too little attention to the systemic risks and suffered badly after the crash in 2008.

By using the intuitive approach of crafting strategy many investors are not aware of the strategic nature of their investments and they make inconsistent decisions. No sound strategy is put in place and there is a big chance for losses.

A crafted strategy lies mostly in the investor's brain without being accurately documented and it is therefore blurred with missing critical elements, such as a clear risk policy. In many cases the investor never develops a plan for implementation and the result is a poorly realized strategy that leads to losses.

By applying a systematic process where alternatives are deliberately developed and evaluated, the investor knows that, to the best of his knowledge, he has chosen the strategy that best fits his strengths and interests and thus has the highest potential for success. This is imperative because the time frame of an investment strategy extends for many years and cannot be switched every year. Moreover, the strategy is not solely related to financial activities and often has a big impact on the personal life of the investor. For example, in the case of Uli, our interview partner from Chapter 5, his strategy to become an investor in unquoted companies in China led to many trips to the region, where he built a circle of friends and developed a special interest in Asian cultures and religions. This was a natural fit for him and appealed to his cultural interests in ways that enriched his life far beyond making good investments.

A formal approach in developing a sound strategy requires the investor to conduct an extensive analysis, to consider different alternatives, and to evaluate them carefully. Most notably, a structured thinking process must be applied to systematically increase the chances of choosing the best strategy with the highest probability of success.

As an outcome of the strategy process, the investor should arrive at a written comprehensive strategy covering all relevant dimensions, which he can consult whenever necessary and use as a sound basis for strategy implementation. The increased awareness also provides the investor with a good foundation when it comes to adapting or changing the strategy. In this manner the danger of inconsistent investments in fields where the investor has too little experience is clearly reduced.

Of course, there are also disadvantages to a formal approach. A systematic strategy process is time-consuming and its execution must be conducted with discipline. There is also a danger that the strategy is logical but does not fit an individual's interests and preferences, and a lack of emotional binding to the strategy can hinder implementation. Finally, the strategy design process is more complex than the crafting strategy process, requiring higher intellectual engagement and commitment.

This chapter examines two principal ways in which investment strategies are developed. Most strategic investors we interviewed used the first path, with their strategy emerging after the repetition of (successful) investment decisions. Because this approach has several crucial shortcomings, we strongly promote a systematic approach that comprehensively addresses all relevant elements that are critical to successful wealth creation.

Chapter 7

WHAT SHOULD AN EFFECTIVE INVESTMENT STRATEGY CONTAIN?

Our practical experience shows that a strategy should be kept as simple as possible while still including the following items:

1. The vision of the investor
2. The core competences the investor intends to build
3. The structure of the investment portfolio
4. Handling threats and risks
5. The networks the investor intends to build and use
6. Guidelines for cash and liquidity
7. Priorities for allocating the investor's resources
8. The legal and tax structure.

THE VISION OF THE INVESTOR

As a first element, the investor should develop and articulate a realistic and credible statement that reflects a deeply rooted vision. Jack Welch, the former chairman of General Electric, notes: "Good business leaders create a vision, articulate the vision, passionately own the vision, and relentlessly drive it to completion"[1] (Bennis and Nanus 1985, p. 87–89).

Investment firms and family offices often articulate a vision, as Aeris Capital does, which captures several interdependent elements that are used to inform its strategy.

> Aeris Capital is the private investment advisor for our principal and the principal's foundation. We take pride in satisfying our principal's objectives through our excellence in performance, modesty and integrity. We aspire to being recognized as the premier address similarly situated families would turn to. Our success is directly related to the level of skill, experience and motivation we and our employees bring to bear in realizing our common vision.[2]

In our interviews we observed that successful investors usually have a clear vision of how they intend to create wealth. The vision can sometimes be very strong, so much so that the investor follows his or her vision with passion and obsession. Rolland-Yves, for example, told us that his vision is to serve the patient by discovering innovative molecules for the treatment of serious medical conditions. Therefore he invests in R&D projects that focus on the development of innovative drugs that contribute to the well-being of patients. He had no interest in investing in capital markets. As he expressed during our interview, "our mission is investment in superior molecules and sharing of benefits." The strategic focus of his investments followed this vision for decades, yielding exceptional performance and resulting in one of the most successful privately held drug development companies in Switzerland.[3]

This example illustrates how a vision should clearly document the strategic direction of the investor. Merely saying, "I want to become rich" is far too general. The vision should clearly define the focus of the investor, leaving room for flexibility and adaptability to allow for unexpected opportunities. In the case of Rolland-Yves the following vision is clearly articulated, "We provide innovative, relevant and accessible therapies for tomorrow's world, through responsible medicine."

THE CORE COMPETENCES THE INVESTOR INTENDS TO BUILD

We have intentionally placed strengths and core competences at the center of our framework because the strategic investor can create wealth only when he or she has outstanding competences in a core field of investment. The investor should create a clear written statement about the core competences needed. Here are some examples:

> To become a successful investor in medical technology I want to have the best know-how in this market.

> I will build outstanding know-how of professional board membership and company management in order to add value to my direct investments.

> I want to build an outstanding capability with regard to quantitative hedge fund management.

The number of core competences an investor can build over a professional lifetime is very limited. In our interviews it became clear that successful investors seldom achieve more than three core competencies during their investment lifetime.

THE STRUCTURE OF THE INVESTMENT PORTFOLIO

A core element of every investment strategy is the structure of the portfolio. Where should the investor put his funds?

Since substantial wealth creation can be achieved only where the investor has outstanding competences, the majority of the funds should be placed in the field where the investor has developed a strong focus. In the example at the beginning of this book, Martin decided to focus on direct investments in unquoted companies, eventually investing 60 percent of his wealth in his focus portfolio of unquoted companies, where he had his main strength and his core competence. The remaining 40 percent of his wealth was in other asset classes, such as cash, real estate, bonds, and stocks.

Figure 7.1   Martin's portfolio structure

Portfolio allocation

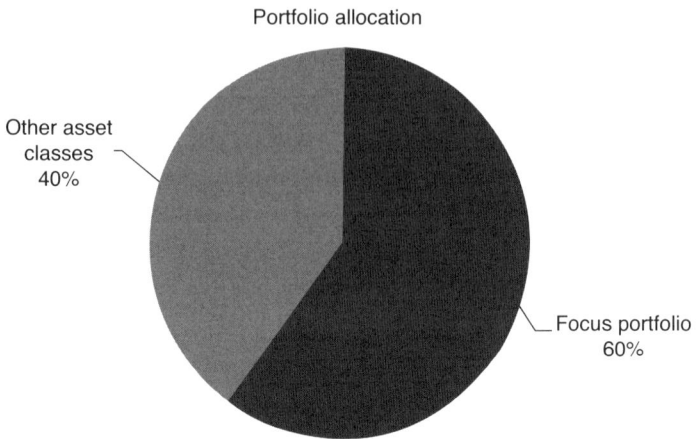

Other asset
classes
40%

Focus portfolio
60%

The focus portfolio is at the center of the investment strategy, in a
field where the investor has developed core competences, enabling him
or her to create wealth through competitive advantage. The remaining
funds can be invested in other asset classes such as cash, bonds, stocks,
real estate, and so on.

The concentration of forces, as represented by the focus portfolio,
may result in a concentration of risk, and the savvy investor should
thus never put all his eggs in one basket. Paul, for example, always
had, besides his focus investments in real estate, a cash position in his
bank account for a certain level of security. Paul could survive a real
estate crash that limited cash flow for quite some time, and crashes
can happen in any asset class. These crashes are unexpected events
(power law events or black swans) with a strong impact, which is why
we urge every investor to create a "security portfolio" with highly liquid safe assets (cash in a savings bank with a sound balance sheet,
bonds of AAA institutions, life insurance, etc.).

What is the optimal size of the security portfolio? It depends on
the specific situation of the investor. A young person can be much
more aggressive with investments because, in the case of failure, he
or she has enough time for a second chance. Older people should
be more conservative. In an ideal case, the security portfolio should

enable the investor to maintain his standard of living during a crash, over a three- to five-year period.[4]

Funds invested in a security portfolio should be exposed to low risk, which usually has the consequence of generating limited returns. Therefore, an investor who has already built wealth should also consider investments in asset classes with higher return potential, such as stocks, high yield bonds, hedge funds, and private equity, adding a greater level of diversification. In this case we consider it prudent to create a third portfolio we call a "diversification portfolio."

Finally, in a free market new opportunities are always emerging, especially through innovation. Even with limited funds an investor can exploit these opportunities to participate in potentially attractive investments, or to experiment in new assets that, at a later stage, could form the basis of a new focus portfolio. We call this fourth portfolio the "opportunity portfolio."

A chart of this portfolio concept is presented in Figure 7.2. An investor should allocate funds to the different portfolios:

Figure 7.2   Example of the overall structure of a portfolio for wealth creation

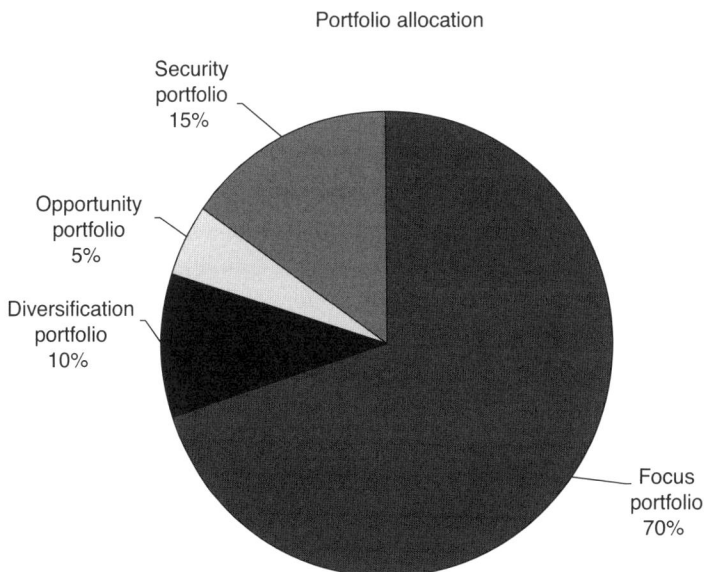

Portfolio allocation

Security portfolio 15%

Opportunity portfolio 5%

Diversification portfolio 10%

Focus portfolio 70%

- Focus portfolio: core of wealth creation
- Security portfolio: enables the investor to survive crashes
- Diversification portfolio: contributes in a limited way to wealth creation and helps to diversify risk
- Opportunity portfolio: exploits special opportunities and potentially creates the basis for future focus investments.

Each portfolio has a specific purpose and characteristics:

The focus portfolio leverages the core competences of the investor and should generate substantial returns. If possible, this portfolio should relate to a field of investment at the beginning of a long life cycle. To achieve high returns the investor must be prepared to invest in assets with low liquidity and at times tolerate considerable risk.

The diversification portfolio should contribute to wealth creation, at least in a limited way. But its key task is wealth preservation through a diversification that also contributes to risk reduction. The investor must recognize that he or she cannot be a specialist in every field and should therefore engage good advisors with insights into investments for the diversification portfolio. The life cycle concept plays a role here since a certain balance with the focus portfolio should be secured. When the focus portfolio contains assets at the beginning of the life cycle, the diversification portfolio should concentrate on large, liquid value companies at the later stage of the life cycle.

The security portfolio allows the investor to maintain his life style during crash (black swan) events. The return on investment is of minor importance because the availability of funds in a crisis, minimal volatility, low risk and high liquidity are the key purposes of the portfolio. Because there are relatively few assets that meet this prerequisite (cash, safe bonds, gold coins or bullion),[5] the investor can use brokers and other consultants for advice in decision making. Asset life cycles are not a factor here.

The opportunity portfolio, in contrast to the security portfolio, should open new perspectives in new fields of investment with potential new options. If the investor is lucky it is possible to achieve outstanding financial results within this portfolio, which is certainly

desirable but not the central objective. Of course, these investments
are highly risky because they are often at the beginning of a life cycle
where the outcomes are not yet clear; therefore a high risk tolerance
is necessary. The investor's competences are not an imperative prerequisite since the opportunity portfolio is a chance to start building
related competences.

Table 7.1 summarizes these descriptions.

This concept of portfolio construction is clearly different from the
classic Markowitz capital market theory. Markowitz uses a combination of different asset classes to construct an "optimal" portfolio. In
our approach, we consider the four portfolios as independent, with
the size of each defined by the needs and preferences of the investor,
and not by a mean-variance portfolio selection model, as in capital
market theory.[6]

Table 7.1 Description of the four portfolios of strategic wealth creation

	Focus	*Diversification*	*Security*	*Opportunity*
Return, wealth creation	Highly important, a must	Important	Of little importance	High return potential desirable
Risk tolerance	High	Low	Very low	Very high
Investor Competencies	Of central importance	Use know-how of brokers or advisors	Use know-how of brokers or advisors	Build new competences
Life cycle	At the beginning	Integrate value companies in later stages of life cycle	Not applicable	Very early stage, emerging
Liquidity	Of little importance	Desirable	Very important	Of little importance
Opening new options	Of lesser importance	Unimportant	Unimportant	Highly important

Examples

To illustrate our portfolio concept in more detail, we describe here some examples of the portfolio structure of different investors.

Example 1: A 43-year-old woman invested in unquoted private companies in 2011. Since her personal wealth was limited she decided to invest most of her fortune in a focus portfolio. Her cash position (security portfolio) was relatively small, but she had some funds in a portfolio of highly liquid stocks (diversification portfolio). In case of a personal crisis, she could liquidate the stock portfolio. She also invested a small amount in Internet companies with outstanding growth potential (opportunity portfolio).

This investor can take considerable risks since she is fairly young. If she fails, she still has many years ahead of her to build a new fortune. Therefore she is able to put 75 percent of her wealth in the focus portfolio.

Figure 7.3   Portfolio structure of a 43-year-old investor

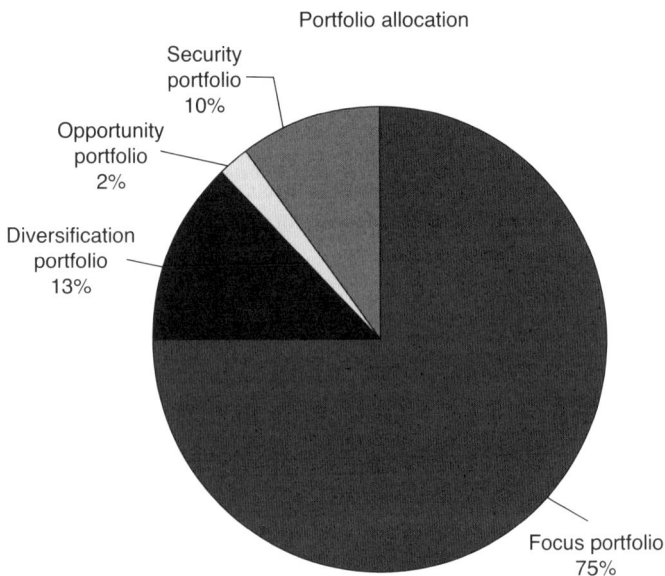

Portfolio allocation

Security portfolio 10%

Opportunity portfolio 2%

Diversification portfolio 13%

Focus portfolio 75%

Example 2: A 52-year-old engineer and investor concentrated on smaller medical technology companies for his focus portfolio, which had yielded a large return. Due to his success with this focus portfolio the investor began to reduce his direct investments and started to build his security and diversification portfolios. In his opportunity portfolio the investor concentrated on fields related to biotechnology.

Figure 7.4   Portfolio structure of a 52-year-old investor

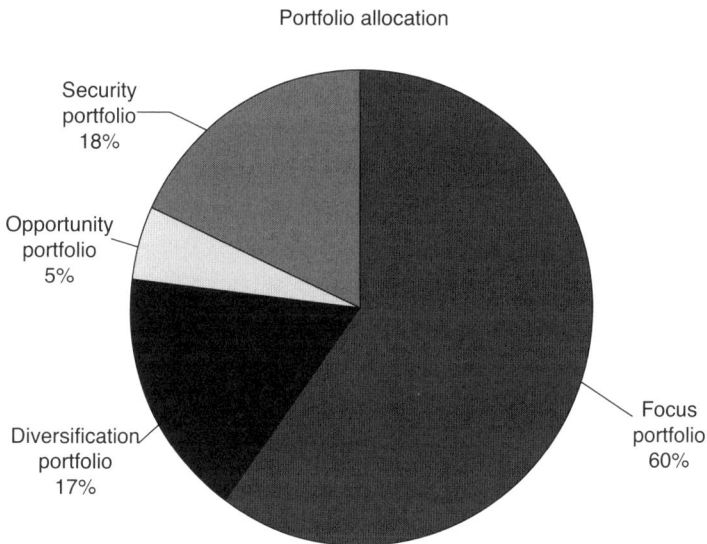

Portfolio allocation

Security portfolio 18%

Opportunity portfolio 5%

Diversification portfolio 17%

Focus portfolio 60%

Example 3: A 63-year-old real estate investor confronted an increasingly problematic situation in the European financial markets after 2008, with an increased risk of a crash in the real estate market. Due to his age the investor started to divest properties in mid-2012, and the importance of his security portfolio increased substantially. The investor decided to build a diversification portfolio in liquid assets. For the opportunity portfolio the investor started to invest in real estate in emerging markets. Due to his age this investor began to build a substantial security and diversification portfolio.

Figure 7.5   Portfolio structure of a 63-year-old real estate investor

Portfolio allocation

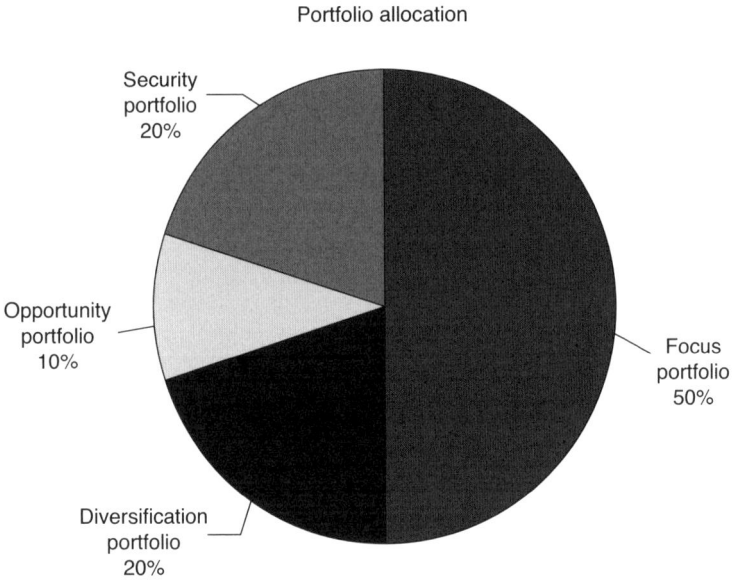

Security
portfolio
20%

Opportunity
portfolio
10%

Focus
portfolio
50%

Diversification
portfolio
20%

From these examples we see how different factors related to the circumstances of the investor can influence the portfolio structure. First, the overall wealth of the investor has to be considered. An investor with only limited funds might be forced to invest a large part of his or her fortune in a focus portfolio. But for an investor who has already built a larger fortune, wealth creation becomes less critical and wealth preservation may become more prominent in the investment strategy, with the security and diversification portfolios becoming proportionally larger.

A second criterion is age. A younger investor can take more risks since, in case of failure, a new start is possible. Therefore, he or she can invest a large part of their fortune in a focus portfolio. Older investors must be more careful. The overarching criterion here is the capability to bear risks.

The third criterion depends on what investment opportunities are available. It does not make sense to invest a considerable part of a fortune in a focus portfolio if – for instance, because of a bear market – there are only limited opportunities.

Another criterion is the investor's competences. A highly competent specialist with outstanding capabilities might be ready to invest a substantial part of his or her assets in a focus portfolio. If the investor is just starting to build core competences, a more prudent approach is advisable.

HANDLING THREATS AND RISKS

Once the portfolio structure has been defined the investor should define his policy on managing threats and risks. A strategy of concentration bears inherently more risks than classic concepts, which is the price for generating the higher returns necessary for wealth creation. Risk policy thus becomes a critical issue and the investor should identify and focus on:

- Key risk factors
- Approaches to control risks, such as research and due diligence
- Building and using reserves
- Guidelines for prudent leverage.

THE NETWORKS THE INVESTOR INTENDS TO BUILD AND USE

To be successful, the investor has to decide which networks he intends to build and develop, and how to nurture and deploy them within the overall investment strategy. These networks may be related to other investors who follow a similar investment strategy – friends, business partners, and others.

Banks and investment advisors can also play an important role in the strategy of every investor. Since almost all investment transactions within the focus portfolio must be performed through bank accounts, the investor needs a strong relationship with one or more banks.

In the portfolio structure, besides the focus portfolio there are three other sub-portfolios that must be created: security, diversification, and opportunity portfolios. Banks and investment advisors can play a key role with regard to these sub-portfolios and contribute to their success since it is they, not the strategic investor, who have the core competences, experience, and know-how for construction and management of these portfolios.

Banks and investment advisors that establish a sound, trusted relationship with the investor support him or her in a broader way that covers all the strategic principles:

- They can support the investor in building core competences with information about new publications, seminars and other events.
- They can identify investment opportunities for the focus portfolio.
- They can support the investor by establishing new network connections that might be of great interest to the investor since these are mostly weak ties (see section on networks in Chapter 5).
- They may advise the investor about differentiation opportunities.
- They can contribute to management of threats and risks given their experience and know-how on general economic trends. The same goes for timing since these professionals can provide unbiased support.

In general, banks and investment advisors can contribute to the success of strategic investing. For example, one of our authors is a member of an investment committee of a family office that follows a strategic investment approach and relies on experts from a global bank for the security and diversification portfolios, as well as other contributions. With fees capped and defined in advance, there is no conflict of interest in engaging advisors who prefer to work with knowledgeable and focused clients who appreciate advice and service.

GUIDELINES FOR CASH AND LIQUIDITY

A careful cash and liquidity plan is mandatory in ensuring solvency, and the investor must at all times know his future cash inflows as well as future cash needs for investments. The purpose of the liquidity plan is to identify bottlenecks as well as cash surpluses that can be used for additional investments. The investor should pay particular attention to avoid liquidity shortage which could force urgent liquidation of assets at lower valuation to provide needed liquidity.

The principle purpose of the security portfolio is to provide liquidity in times of crisis. In this portfolio the investor allocates highly secure assets, such as cash in bank accounts, money market funds, (AAA) bonds, and gold coins or bullion. In times of financial crisis or geographical turmoil the investor should pay particular attention to protecting cash and liquidity, for example by addressing the risk associated with the balance sheet of the depository bank where the assets are held, as well as their legal jurisdiction. The 2008 financial crisis, for example, was a critical time when investor diligence was required to protect cash and liquidity. If the investor held his security portfolio at Lehman Brothers, for example, he would have potentially lost significant cash and liquidity at a time when they could have been most needed. To mitigate this risk, some investors spend considerable effort to evaluate the balance sheet risk of their banks and move their security portfolios to smaller regional banks with solid balance sheets and low exposure to financial risk.

PRIORITIES FOR THE ALLOCATION OF INVESTOR RESOURCES

The essence of strategy is the optimal deployment of available resources. The investor must specify and prioritize his resources including:

- Human resources – The investor must prioritize his or her personal time in order to achieve optimum results.
- Technology resources – The investor must be clear on how he or she intends to leverage technology.
- Financial resources – The investor must determine the availability and prioritize deployment of financial resources.

For individual investors, personal time is usually the most valuable and scarce resource to be prioritized and used efficiently. In other cases, such as when an investor concentrates on quantitative investment concepts, technology may become a major concern.

THE LEGAL AND TAX STRUCTURE

Legal dimensions nearly always have a material effect on wealth creation, or rather in hampering wealth creation. Advisors should be consulted early when drafting a strategy to take into account the legal and tax implications of portfolio structures and investments, as they relate to the specific circumstances of the investor. In a world of increasing complexity it is imperative to proactively monitor the evolution of the legal and tax environment to ensure compliance and optimization of portfolio performance.

Example

We have purposely kept discussions about strategic decisions statements brief because in our opinion it is more effective to keep the strategy as simple as possible. To illustrate, below is an example of a simple outline of an investment strategy for a 42-year-old marketing consultant with a net worth of US $2 million.

Table 7.2 Example of a simple investment strategy outline

Vision	I want to become a successful investor in small, marketing oriented private companies and support the dynamic growth of these companies
Core Competences	(a) Ability to identify, evaluate and realize attractive direct investments in the field of small marketing services companies.
	(b) A strong network that provides knowledge and access to attractive small marketing companies.
	(c) Ability to ensure the development of the invested companies through active board membership.
Portfolio Structure	(a) Focus portfolio:
	70% to 80% of net worth;
	Direct investments in small, marketing oriented companies.
	(b) Security portfolio:
	10% to 15% of net worth;
	cash in the equivalent of personal expenditure of two years;
	own home with the possibility of increasing mortgage if one day necessary.
	(c) Diversification portfolio:
	5% to 10% of net worth;
	highly liquid quoted stocks.
	(d) Opportunity portfolio:
	2% to 3% of net worth;
	quoted stocks of marketing oriented Internet companies.
Risk Policy	Extensive observation of direct investments through participation on the board of portfolio companies; limited leverage on own house (mortgage).
Networks	Active membership as board member of the regional marketing club; active lecturing at marketing events; building contacts to selected M&A companies.
Cash and Liquidity Policy	Regular cash flows from continuous consulting income; little dividend income in order to save taxes; create a limited liquidity cushion through unused bank credit pledge.
Resource Allocation	Concentrate on board activity of portfolio companies; systematically build own network; improve competence with regard to due diligence and company valuation.
Legal and Tax Structure	Create a tax efficient holding company in which all direct investments are consolidated.

Chapter 8

PUTTING THE PROCESS OF STRATEGIC INVESTING INTO PRACTICE

ESSENTIAL CONSIDERATIONS

Recapping our key findings, we emphasize that:

1. Wealth cannot be created by following traditional investment advice. If you invest according to the traditional diversification concepts and capital market theory promoted by the finance industry, you may be able to preserve wealth or, in the best case, generate marginal returns.

2. To create wealth an investor must apply strategic concepts to develop an investment strategy that:
   - builds on investor strengths and core competencies
   - exploits opportunities
   - uses networks
   - incorporates an investment approach that differentiates the investor from others
   - prevents threats and handles risks appropriately

- observes trends and cycles and invests accordingly
- is executed with high efficiency

The strategic investor must build strengths and core competencies, and use available resources (personal time, finances, IT, and so on) in a concentrated manner.

3. It is advisable to develop the strategy through a formal process, as illustrated in Figure 8.1.

Figure 8.1 The formal process of strategic investing. In each step the "Strategic Framework" (see Figure 5.1) is applied as a guideline

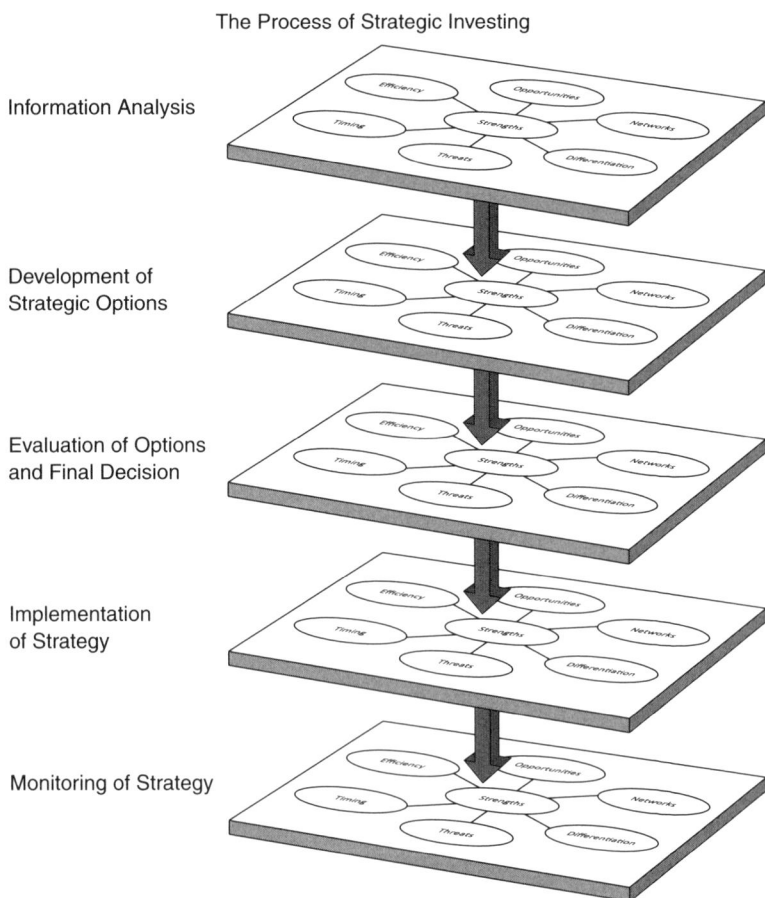

The Process of Strategic Investing

Information Analysis

Development of Strategic Options

Evaluation of Options and Final Decision

Implementation of Strategy

Monitoring of Strategy

KEY QUESTIONS TO ASK – INFORMATION ANALYSIS

Before defining a strategy every strategist must make a situation assessment of opponents, environment, and other factors using checklists developed for this purpose. For instance, many of the successful investors we interviewed used a formal analysis of future macroeconomic trends in relation to gross domestic product, exchange rates, income distribution, and employment.

But since almost unlimited information is available today, the investor needs guidance to identify the most useful information. Asking key questions during the process of information analysis can help assure identifying the critical information needed, namely:

1. What are my key strengths? What do I have a passion for? Where are my real interests?
2. Which fields of investment (such as asset classes, industries, and geographical areas) have outstanding opportunities?
3. What networks can I use?
4. Where can I differentiate myself from other investors? Where can I achieve a competitive edge?
5. Where are the critical threats and risks?
6. Which fields of investment are attractive from a timing point of view (overall trends, cycles)?
7. What are the costs of key strategic options?

Questions on strengths

An investor reading this book has typically some sort of knowledge and experience about investing along with an excess of information from newspapers, TV, and other media. Where does he or she start? The framework presented in this book has been designed to provide guidance.

Strategic success can only be achieved when the investor has core competencies related to his strengths, allowing him to make the right operational decisions. The investment universe is highly competitive and other investors, and legions of professional analysts and experts, also have core competencies. Therefore, building core competencies is quite a challenge, and psychological issues become relevant. In our interviews we saw that successful investors, in almost all cases, had a passion for their strategy suggesting that a strong affinity to a field of investment is a key success factor.

This is why every strategic information analysis should start with the strengths, interests and passions of the investor. The investor should ask:

- Where do I have a special know-how? What are my special capabilities?
- What would I like to do for future investments? Where do my personal interests lie? What do I find fun?
- What are my passions? What excites me? Where could I develop such a passion?

Analyzing these questions is not a mechanical process but a thought process that requires reflection, insight, and discussing the issues with people who know you well and whose judgment you trust.

Questions on opportunities

To successfully develop a wealth-generating strategy an investor needs a long-term perspective, analyzing global and regional mega-trends, and identifying attractive opportunities. Seeking advice from financial service providers or searching Bloomberg has limited value in this process because of the short-term focus of these sources.

Hundreds of books and publications, such as *2052: A Global Fore-cast for the Next Forty Years,* can provide insights into new trends. For example, in *2052* the author analyzes how our economies, energy supplies, natural resources, climate, food, fisheries, military, political divisions, and cities will take shape over the coming decades.[1]

But which opportunities are important for a specific investor? To begin, the investor should rank opportunities according to the following three categories, using his strengths as the key criterion:

First, are there opportunities that match the strengths of the investor?

Second, are there opportunities that are neutral and do not match the investor's strengths?

Third, are there opportunities that the investor has no relationship with yet?

Careful analysis of the opportunity landscape should yield a ranking of opportunities that can be used for developing the strategy.

Questions on networks

Networks are a key element for strategic success and the investor should consider the following questions:

- What networks are available to me? In what fields of investment?
- What potential networks can I build? In what fields of investment?
- Which networks can help me to differentiate for competitive advantage?
- What kinds of information can the network provide me as an investor?
- How can I build the proper networks for my core competencies and focus portfolio?
- How can I nurture and maintain a two-way network?

Answers to these questions should help the investor identify and evaluate his approach in developing effective networks to support his strategy.

Questions on differentiation

Differentiation is one of the most difficult principles because so many investors occupy the investment landscape, making it hard to find a viable niche. But this difficulty is also an opportunity since, if the investor does find a niche with little competition, he may be able to develop strong differentiation that can be extremely interesting. The investor should begin with scanning the field of investments identified in his information analysis on strengths and opportunities. Questions to be asked include:

- In which fields of investment can I differentiate myself?
- Where is there little competition?
- How can I develop a unique investment concept?
- What are the prerequisites for successful differentiation?
- What are the core competencies required to build a unique investment concept that differentiates me as an investor?
- How should I build the core competencies that differentiate me as an investor?

Questions on threats and risks

The investor should further analyze the fields of investment identified in his information analysis regarding strengths and opportunities, from the perspective of threats and risks. Questions to be answered include:

- What are the real threats and risks I, as an investor, am likely to confront in the coming years?
- How can I handle these threats and risks?
- What mechanisms must I adopt to avoid threats and risks during the investment life cycle?

Questions on timing

It would be wrong to concentrate on a field of investment at the peak of its life cycle because investments would be made at high valuations in a declining market. Therefore the time perspective has to be carefully analyzed by asking key questions:

- Where do these fields of investment stand in their life cycle?
- What is my investment horizon?
- How are these fields of investment expected to evolve from a megatrend point of view?
- What are the guidelines for successful timing?
- Under what circumstances should a strategy be flexible?
- Are there lessons in history related to timing of investments?
- What are the time-related factors that may affect my decisions over the life cycle of investments?

Questions on efficiency

Efficiency has a critical impact on the success of an investment strategy. Therefore, the investor must analyze costs and other efficiency factors with regard to the main strategic directions identified, asking these questions:

- What are the investment fees associated with the potential fields of investment?
- Are there ways to realize the investment strategy efficiently?
- What are the dimensions of efficiency when implementing the strategy?
- What are the efficiency related factors affecting the strategic investment operations? How can they be enhanced?

Practical considerations

How should the information analysis be conducted? How much time should be invested?

One easy way is to record the answers immediately and have a list within hours. But we know from experience this would be too easy and that the investor will find only basic answers to some of the questions.

We prefer an iterative process where a relatively concentrated information analysis is performed at the first stage, lasting over days or weeks, to gain a clear understanding. From here the investor can think about strategic options by further analyzing the issues.

DEVELOPING OPTIONS AS A STEP TO SUCCESS

Since deciding on an effective strategy is so important to the success of the investor, and since the risk of failure is real, we are convinced that a formal application of the strategy development process is crucial. Only after a thorough formal information analysis should the investor think about the strategic options open to him or her.

Ralph, our example in Chapter 6, did not consider just one alternative but several options. One was concentrating on hedge funds, another was aimed at private equity, and a third option was direct investments. The advantage of systematic thinking about alternatives is that it enhances the probability of finding a good strategy. Often the best ideas emerge only after some time, and once the most obvious ideas are eliminated. The same goes for strategy formulation. If only the most obvious strategy is selected there is the danger that the best strategy is missed.

Moreover, if the investor sticks to the most obvious strategy, there is always a feeling that there could be a better one, which hinders implementation of the strategy. Even more dangerous is if the investor has not clearly defined the strategy, and thus makes investments that do not fit, which can negatively affect his performance.

Creating alternative options

The result of the first step, the information analysis, is a list of findings. Next the investor should ask what are the most important strengths that he can leverage at the core of his investment strategy? Martin, for example, considered his know-how as a manager and CFO as his crucial strengths. He selected the strategy that made best use of these strengths, concluding that direct investments in private companies was the right field of investment for him.

In many cases we have seen that at this stage the investor stops thinking of alternatives, but we believe it is worth spending sufficient time to think about options. This is a critical point because there may be other strengths on which a better strategy could be built. Martin, for example, had access to private equity management companies, and he could have chosen private equity fund investments rather than direct investments in his strategy.

Depending on the circumstances there may also be cases where the investor's core strengths do not fit the opportunity landscape. For instance, an investor living in a region affected by the real estate collapse of 2008 might have acquired extensive know-how in real estate but, due to the downturn in the real estate cycle, this know-how may be useless for many years. In such cases, or in cases where the investor does not have clear strengths, other options have to be developed. For example, opportunities can serve as a starting point. The investor must decide which opportunities to concentrate on, and then build specific strengths and core competencies that fit the strategic option. Similarly, other elements of the strategic framework, such as networks, differentiation, or timing, can be used to generate strategic options. If, for example, the investor has a strong network that can provide unique insights and access to a specific field of investment, he may choose to build the strategy around this strength.

Of course, the process of developing options cannot be performed in a few minutes or hours and may require significant effort to generate alternatives. Depending on the individual situation it may be necessary to do extensive research and analysis, and this step could take weeks or months. In conclusion, the investor must have a set of strategic options that need to be evaluated.

THE MOMENT OF TRUTH – EVALUATING OPTIONS
AND MAKING DECISIONS

The question now is how to evaluate the options and make the final decision. Management science has developed several methods for this, of which the easiest is to specify the pros and cons of each option. One can also define specific criteria and measure each option against the criteria. Sophisticated value grading charts or models can quantify potential risks and returns. Kahneman stresses that simple and equally weighted methods with about six criteria produce good results. [2]

From our experience, a thought process is needed more than a (mechanical) evaluation method. Extensive analysis and debate should lead to a deeper understanding of the decision-making process and thus to a sound decision that is custom-made for the investor's specific circumstances. Asking the right questions and using the framework presented here will help the investor in generating and evaluating his strategic options. The criteria to be considered lead to the following questions:

- To what extent does each considered strategic option build on (existing) strengths? Can important strengths/core competencies be built with relative ease? Which strategy would I really enjoy implementing? For which strategy do I have, or could I develop, a passion?
- To what extent does each of the alternative strategies exploit opportunities? How big are these opportunities?
- To what extent does each alternative make use of existing networks? Can strong new networks be built specifically for the strategic option?
- Does the option allow a differentiated approach to investing?
- Does the strategic option avoid threats? Can risks be controlled?

- Which of the alternative strategies would be the most successful from a timing point of view? Does it aim at an emerging life cycle?
- Can the strategic option be realized at reasonable costs? What about opportunity costs?

We see the stages of information analysis, development of alternatives, and deciding on the strategy not as a linear process but rather as an iterative one. It may be necessary to analyze additional new information along the way as other ideas with regard to new options emerge.

Finally, to clarify his vision, an investor should put the strategy on paper with specific subtitles which force him to create an integrated strategy by thinking about all dimensions of creating wealth.

THE HARD WORK – IMPLEMENTING THE STRATEGY

Until now the whole strategy process has been rather abstract. Besides information processing, no action has been taken and not a cent invested. In implementing the strategy, however, many actions must be taken and many things may go wrong.

A main danger is that the investor rushes too fast into making the first investments. To make good investment decisions the investor must first ensure that the necessary core competencies are available, that he is able to access a strong network, and that he has sufficiently evaluated the investment landscape to identify the most suitable investment opportunities. Therefore, before implementing the strategy, the investor must identify and plan for actions to undertake, otherwise the risk of failure is considerable.

To build the necessary strengths and core competencies, the investor must carefully analyze his actual knowledge and then specify the core competencies needed for a successful launch and implementation. For instance, if the investor has chosen commercial real estate for the focus portfolio, he must acquire a deep understanding of the real estate investment process, including the ability to judge the offering of different real estate outfits. Legal, due diligence, and financial knowledge must be acquired to understand and implement investments successfully. The investor must establish contacts with experienced persons in the focus investment field and decide which organizations (banks, advisors) to collaborate with.

These actions can be planned in a rational way, but most of the problems with implementing a strategy are psychological. Let us take as a simple example an investor who intends to concentrate on private equity. To build the necessary core competencies he or she must attend seminars, for a start. Because these new actions may be unfamiliar there is often considerable uncertainty and uneasiness, so psychological barriers have to be overcome. The investor will need to meet many new people, which may be uncomfortable depending on his temperament and social inclinations. Moreover, the cost of travel, seminars, etc. may be an expenditure that is undertaken reluctantly. In order to overcome potential psychological barriers, the strategy must be planned carefully and executed with discipline.

Because the investor should apply an approach that differentiates him or her from other investors, it is not advisable to follow the most obvious or usual route. More creative, newer solutions have to be developed.

For threats and risks, the investor must develop the capability to identify, quantify, and mitigate them efficiently and effectively. Also challenging is the experience and capability to recognize life cycles for correct timing, and the investor should also develop the capacity to monitor and judge cycles with accuracy. Finally, the investor must be able to invest at reasonable cost by studying the costs related to investments as well as possible opportunity costs.

Thus the investor must ask what actions are necessary to build competencies by establishing a list of actions, defining priorities, and specifying the time frame in which these actions must be accomplished. Action plans have to be established not only for building competencies but also for addressing operational issues such as identifying specific investment opportunities.

At this point the investor should have several action plans to implement the strategy. Even the best action plan is worthless if not realized. Implementation of the strategy can last several months or years, and success can only be realized with a lot of discipline and devotion. Therefore, the ultimate question for becoming a successful strategic investor is whether the individual is willing to bear the challenges related to this endeavor.

ENSURING SUCCESS – STRATEGIC CONTROL

The final stage in the strategy process is control. Since action plans cannot be carried out without friction, implementation of the strategy must be carefully monitored. The investor should develop a process for monitoring implementation on a regular basis, and adapt the strategy if necessary. It might be useful to begin with answering the following questions:

- Is the information acquired in the information analysis still valid?
- How have the assumptions changed? Are they still valid?
- Is the strategy being implemented as planned?
- Are there unexpected difficulties?
- Must the strategy be adapted due to unexpected realities?

Since future developments rarely evolve as planned, these questions must be asked and answered in an ongoing process.

Chapter 9

PUTTING EVERYTHING TOGETHER

We would like to end this book with an example of a highly successful strategic investor, going back to the 1970s and lasting about 25 years. While we live in a very different global environment today, this example is used to illustrate that the guiding strategic principles are timeless, having been used for over 3000 years.

A FINAL STORY: HENRY'S SUCCESS

Henry entered a well-known European university in the 1970s and occasionally worked part-time to make money. After graduating with an MBA he joined a major accounting firm but resigned after six months, saying "work in an auditing company is boring." He began a new job with a large insurance company but again left after a few months because the work did not satisfy him. His next job was with a small bank in London where he stayed for two years, although he never enjoyed working there. He realized that, long-term, he did not want to work for someone else but wanted to become an independent investor. He knew this would not be possible with his limited knowledge and that he had to improve his skills in investments and company management. He decided, "the best place to learn about management is in a leading management consulting company."

In the late 1970s Henry contacted the managing partner of a leading consulting firm and requested to work for them. The partner checked Henry's credentials, concluding that he would not meet their requirements and the application was declined. Henry did not give up and contacted other offices of the same firm in Germany, still with no success. Finally, he took the initiative to meet one of the managing partners at the Munich office and told him: "I decided to work for your firm, but your colleagues do not want to hire me as a regular consultant. Therefore, I am ready to work for you for free, and you just have to pay me whatever you like if you are satisfied with my work." This impressed the managing partner and Henry was allowed to work at the Munich office. He told us later that he worked very diligently and, due to his excellent performance, was hired as a consultant and stayed with the company for three years.

When he believed he had learned enough about company management, Henry decided to look for a new job, researching which industry might be most suitable for achieving his objective of becoming an independent investor. He decided not to apply for vacancies but to identify several companies and, again, approached the firms directly. With excellent testimonials from his boss at the consulting firm he had worked with, he was hired by a well-known family office and over the next two years focused on learning about investment management.

In the early 1980s Henry learned about the success of a company, Kohlberg, Kravis, Roberts (KKR), a New York firm which was applying a new model at the forefront of private investments. Through leverage buyouts KKR was making significant profits, and Henry wanted to emulate this innovative investment approach in Europe.

By mid-1980s Henry felt that he had the necessary know-how and core competencies to apply the concept of leverage buyouts. He had already identified a company to buy, a specialty publisher in the field of natural science with a turnover of DEM 21 million and a net profit of DEM 2 million. The two owners were prepared to sell the company for DEM 20 million. While a P/E Ratio of 10 was (for a private company) quite expensive, Henry carried out a thorough analysis of the company. He found that for many years the two owners had not actually worked in the company, but had enjoyed life in Florida while collecting about DEM 2 million as salary and bonus every year. Moreover, because nobody really managed the company, an additional DEM 2 million could easily be saved. Therefore, Henry predicted that after the buyout the actual profit would be not two but six million, and thus the P/E Ratio would be less than 4, making the acquisition price very reasonable. In addition, several employees had ideas for new projects that could improve sales considerably.

This investment was extremely successful, and with new development projects and other smaller acquisitions a turnover of over DEM 80 million was achieved with a profit margin of 25 percent in less than three years!

With these excellent results, Henry was able to obtain new loans from the bank and he began to look for new investments in another promising field he had identified. Companies specializing in factory maintenance could be bought at very low prices, and the sector promised excellent opportunity for leverage buyout. With new acquisitions, the consolidated revenue of Henry's investments soon increased above DEM 300 million, with excellent margins. In the final analysis, Henry had achieved an Internal Rate of Return of more than 50 percent, enabling him to create considerable wealth.

If we analyze this story from a strategic perspective we see that Henry applied (sometimes intuitively) most elements of the strategic framework for wealth creation. First, he built core competences, especially in management, finance, and corporate acquisitions. Second, he identified the emergence of the European buyout market as a tremendous opportunity since companies could be bought at prices that today's buyout companies can only dream of.

Third, beginning with his activities with the family office, Henry was able to build a strong network, and his contacts with the small but innovative bank in Munich proved very helpful. Because the buyout concept was almost unknown in Europe at this time, most banks were not willing to provide financing for deals, but the Munich bank understood the new concept and provided the necessary credit.

Fourth, Henry applied a highly differentiated approach. In the early 1980s, most acquisitions were made as proprietary deals with no competitive bidders.

Fifth, he applied thorough risk management. The companies were analyzed carefully and sound supervisory systems were implemented.

And finally, the timing of the strategy was perfect. Henry entered the European leveraged buyout market at the beginning of its life cycle. Regarding efficiency, his buyout company had only two partners, a secretary and no rental of formal offices.

Whether deliberately or unconsciously, Henry applied all the strategic principles of the framework effectively. He formulated a vision to become an independent entrepreneur/investor and he realized the importance of building strengths. During his activity in the family office he considered alternatives, becoming a direct investor or creating a private equity fund. Application of the strategic principles empowered him to realize his vision, and he became one of the most successful alumni of his university, retiring early thanks to his wealth.

We use this final example to show how the principles of the strategic framework can help to secure financial success. But the true value of the framework only becomes evident if we combine the framework with an overall strategy process.

APPLYING THE FRAMEWORK TO ALL ASPECTS OF WEALTH CREATION

The framework provides a structure that can be used at all stages of the strategy process:

- During the information analysis it helps to raise the right questions.
- In the second stage it helps to define strategic options.
- It can facilitate evaluating strategic options when the principles in the framework are used as criteria.
- At implementation it guides correct, important actions.
- Every strategy must be monitored and the framework highlights critical areas that must be controlled.

The seven principles we integrated in the framework are the most important ones and provide strong guidance for developing and implementing the strategy. If an investor follows these seven principles the probability of making fundamental mistakes will be substantially reduced.

FINAL REMARKS ON THIS NEW APPROACH

Books on investing are usually written by finance professionals or academicians in finance, building on investment theory and practice. In our research, interviews, and writing this book, the objective of our team has been to apply a broader knowledge of strategy and approach the subject of wealth creation from a different perspective. At the intersection of the fields of strategy and finance we have elucidated key strategic principles that empower successful investors in their journey of wealth creation. Our objective has been to create discontinuity by offering creative new insights to empower the strategic investor.

APPENDICES

APPENDIX 1   WEALTH CREATION

In this book we have concentrated on one specific way to create wealth, namely by being a strategic investor, although there are many other ways to create wealth. In order to position our approach we would like to provide an overview of the most important ways to create wealth.

Figure A.1   Wealth Creation

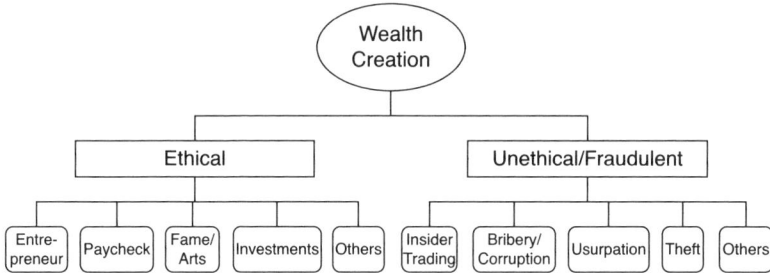

Source: Authors.

From our perspective there are two principal concepts, ethical and unethical. We mention unethical concepts in order to be systematic; unethical or fraudulent methods are not discussed in this book.

- A first option is to become an entrepreneur and create wealth by growing a business. From a statistical point of view this is probably the method that occurs the most.
- Another possibility is to become a senior manager with an outstanding remuneration.

- Becoming a top artist, sportsman / sportswoman, or famous person is yet another way.
- In our book, we concentrate on a fourth way, namely by creating wealth through strategic investing. Please note, that in contrast to the entrepreneur who devotes all of his time to his own company, the strategic investor usually has other activities besides investing.
- Finally, there are other possibilities that should be mentioned, such as inheriting, marrying a rich spouse, and so on.

But let us take a closer look at ethical concepts. As a matter of fact several options exist but, in general, it is obvious that wealth creation is not an easy task. An entrepreneur must be willing to work intelligently and extremely hard for a long time, mostly decades. It is well known that top management positions can usually only be achieved with outstanding capabilities, such as know-how, political sensitivity and hard work. The same goes for artists, sportsmen / sportswomen and other celebrities. And there are other characteristics applicable to all of these options; they are all linked to (often considerable) risks and also to luck (sometimes a lot).

APPENDIX 2   DESCRIPTION OF INTERVIEW PARTNERS

Name	Description
Chris	Chris (who wants to stay anonymous) was originally a highly successful management consultant who became a professional investor in the early 2000s
Carlo	Carlo (who wants to stay anonymous) is a very successful private investor
Christian and Florence	Christian and Florence Jauch have investments in real estate with special services, such as refurbishing the acquired flats in Geneva
Dominique	Dominique (who wants to stay anonymous) is one of the very successful strategic investors in the field of medical technology in Switzerland

Continued

Name	Description
Uwe	Uwe Feuersenger, CEO and Chairman of Aeris Capital, the family office of a SAP co-founder
Henry	Henry (who wants to stay anonymous), a private investor and founder of a private equity fund
Urs	Urs Hammer was chairman and CEO of McDonald's in Switzerland
Martin	Martin (who wants to stay anonymous) began his career as a certified public accountant in the late 1970s. In the 1980s, he accepted the position of CFO in a mid-size company
Joachim	Dr. Joachim Schoss, serial Internet entrepreneur and private investor
Christian	Christian Jenny, leading Jaguar sportscar collector
Jeremy	Jeremy, a real estate investor in Atlanta
Rolland-Yves	Dr. Rolland-Yves Mauvernay, one of the very successful strategic investors in the field of biotechnology in Switzerland
Ralph	Ralph (who wants to stay anonymous), in the 1980s was active as an assistant professor in mathematics. Later on he founded his own company that specialized in banking software
Rudi	Rudi, (who passed away in the 1970s) was a young clerk in a small town in Switzerland, ten miles from the German border after WWII
Paul	Paul (who wants to stay anonymous), worked for a few years in a large electrical installation company. He started his own business thirty years ago in a small European town and became a successful real estate investor
William	William (who wants to stay anonymous) is an employee of a UK bank. He worked in the finance industry in the late 1980s and was responsible for his clients' investments
Pühringer	Pühringer Gruppe, is a successful family office, asset manager and foundation in Austria / Switzerland
Uli	Dr. Uli Sigg, was Swiss Ambassador to China who later became a highly successful private investor and art collector

APPENDIX 3   INFORMATION ANALYSIS

Checklist for an environment analysis

Ecological
Environment
	• Availability of energy
	  - gasoline
	  - natural gas
	  - electricity
	  - coal
	  - other sources of energy
	• Availability of raw materials
	• Trends in environmental protection
	  - awareness of the environment
	  - environmental load
	  - legislation for environmental protection
	• Recycling
	  - availability of recycled materials
	  - cost of recycling

Technology	• Production technology
	  - trends in process technology
	  - innovation potential
	  - automation/process control
	• Production innovation
	  - development trends in production technologies
	  • hardware
	  • software
	  - innovation potential
	• Technology of substitution
	  - possible innovations
	  - cost trends
	• Recycling technology

Economy	• Trends of GNP in the relevant countries
	• Development of international trade
	  - exchange of goods
	  - economic integration
	  - protectionism
	• Balance of payments and exchange trends
	• Expected rate of inflation
	• Capital market trends
	• Employment trends
	• Expected capital investment trends
	• Expected fluctuations in business activities
	  - frequency
	  - intensity
	• Development of specific relevant sectors of the economy

Continued

Checklist for an environment analysis

Demographic and socio-psychological trends	• Population development in the relevant countries
	  - general trends
	  - development of important population groups
	  - migration
	• Socio-psychological tendencies
	  - work ethics
	  - propensity to save
	  - leisure preferences
	  - attitude to the economy
	  - attitude to automation
	  - attitude to important raw materials
	  - attitude to important products

Politics and Law	• Global political trends
	  - East vs. West
	  - North vs. South
	  - general danger of local or international conflicts
	  - market position of raw producers
	• Political developments in relevant countries
	• Trends in economic policies
	• Trends in social and labor legislation
	• Role and influence of labor unions
	• Companies' freedom of action

Reference: Puempin, Cuno, 1981, *The Practice of Strategic Management*, 25–26.

NOTES

2 WHY TRADITIONAL INVESTMENT MODELS DON'T WORK

1. Akerlof, George, and Robert Shiller, 2009, *Animal Spirits: How Human Psychology Drives the Economy, and Why It Matters for Global Capitalism* (Princeton University Press), 131.
2. Dimson, Elroy, Marsh Paul, Staunton Mike, McGinnie Paul, and Wilmot Jonathan, 2014, Credit Suisse Global Investment Returns Yearbook, *Research Institute*, 46–58.
3. Cuthbertson, Keith, Nitzsche Dirk, and O'Sullivan Niall, 2010, Mutual Fund Performance Measurement and Evidence, *Financial Markets, Institutions and Instruments,* Vol. 19, 1.
4. Fernandez, Pablo, and Del Campo Javier, 2010, *Return of Mutual Funds in Spain 1991–2009,* Working Paper Series, IESE.
5. Thornburg Investment Management, 2013, *A Study of Real Real Returns, Strategies for Building Real Wealth*, Vol. 20, 1–4.
6. Ross, Stephan, Westerfield Randolph, and Jaffe Jeffrey, 2010, *Corporate Finance*, 247–249.
7. Brealey, Richard, and Myers Stewart, 2010, *Principles of Corporate Finance*, 214.
8. One of these concepts is value at risk, which is a risk assessment tool that measures the probability that the value of an asset or portfolio will drop below a specified level in a particular time period. (Gajek, Lestaw, and Ostaszewski Krzystof, 2005, *Financial Risk Management for Pension Plans*, 333–335.)
9. Davidsson, Markus, 2012, Large Impact Events and Finance, *Accounting and Finance Research*, Vol. 1, No. 1, 95–97.
10. Farmer, Doyne, and Geanakoplos John, 2008, *Power Laws in Economics and Elsewhere*, 5–7.
11. Mandlebrot, Benoit, and Hudson Richard, 2008, *The (Mis)behavior of Markets,* Profile Books, 523–537.

12. Puempin, Cuno, and Maurice Pedergnana, 2008, *Strategisches Investment Management*, 24–26.
13. Taleb, Nassim, 2010, *The Black Swan: The Impact of the Highly Improbable* (Random House Trade Paper, New York), 211.
14. Álvarez-Nogal, Carlos, and Chamley Cristophe, 2011, Debt Policy under Constraints between Philip II, the Cortes and Genoese Bankers, Working Paper, Universidad Carlos III de Madrid, 11.
15. Groseclose, Elgin, 1934, *Man and Money: A Survey of Monetary Experience*, 106–108.
16. Ferguson, Niall, 2009, *The Ascent of Money: A Financial History of the World*, 127–132.
17. In 1990, Harry Markowitz, William Sharpe, and Merton Miller, won the Nobel Prize in economics for their contribution to the theory of financial economics. Markowitz is best known for his contributions to the theory of portfolio choice; Sharpe, for his contributions to the capital asset pricing model; and Miller, for his contributions to the theory of corporate finance.
18. Mauldin, John, and Tepper Jonathan, 2013, *Endgame: The End of the Debt Supercycle and How It Changes Everything* (Wiley), 86, 206, 207.
19. Gross, Bill, 2012, *Investment Outlook: The Lending Lindy*, PIMCO.

3   THE INVESTOR BACK AT THE CORE OF INVESTING: LESSONS FROM A CFO – PART 2

1. ETF is an Exchange-Traded Fund, a security that tracks an index, a commodity or a basket of assets like an index fund, but trades like a stock on an exchange. ETFs go through price changes throughout the day as they are bought and sold. (Board of Financial Stability, 2011, Potential financial stability issues arising from recent trends in Exchange-Traded Funds (ETFs), 1–4.)
2. At a time when traditional banking models are under increasing pressure and scrutiny, innovative banks can still play an important role in an investor's approach to his or her wealth creation as described in later chapters.

4   THE ESSENCE OF STRATEGY

1. Chua Amy, 2009, *The Day of the Empire: How Hyperpowers Rise to Global Dominance – and Why They Fall,* First Anchor Books Edition.

2. Battle of Salamis, *Encyclopedia Britannica Online*, Retrieved October 15, 2012.
3. Tzu, Sun, 2011, *The Science of Sun Tzu*, scienceofstrategy.org
4. Zhanghong, Ru, and Zhang Xiao, 1970, *Chinese Characters History Lessons*, Vol. 1, 1–3.
5. Tzu, Sun, 1910, *The Art of War: The Oldest Military Treatise in the War*, 71–157.
6. Noble, Thomas, Strauss Barry, Osheim Duane, Neuschel Kristen, and Accompo Elinor, 2007, *Western Civilization: Beyond Boundaries.*
7. Jomini, Antoine-Henri, 2001, *Précis de l'Art de la Guerre*, Perrin.
8. Clausewitz, Carl V., 1832, *Vom Kriege*, Dummlers Verlag.
9. Forczyk, Robert, 2010, *Erich von Manstein: The Background, Strategies, Tactics and Battlefield Experiences of the Greatest Commanders of History*, Osprey Publishing.
10. Royle, Trevor, 2010, *Montgomery: Lessons in Leadership from the Soldier's General*, Palgrave Macmillan.
11. Liddell Hart, Basil Henry, 1943, *Thoughts on War.*
12. British Defence Doctrine, 2011, Joint Doctrine Publication 0–01, Ministry of Defence.
13. Clausewitz, Carl V., 1942, *Principles of War*, 15–18.
14. Gale, Bradley, and Buzzell Robert, 1987, *The Pims Principles: Linking Strategy to Performance*, Macmillan USA.
15. Porter, Michael, 1980, *Competitive Strategy: Techniques for Analyzing Industries and Competitors*, Free Press.
16. Puempin, Cuno, 1987, *The Essence of Corporate Strategy*, Gower Business Enterprise Series.
17. Puempin, Cuno, 1991, *How World Class Companies became World Class*, Gower Publishing Company.
18. Porter, Michael, 1997, *How Competitive Forces Shape Strategy.*

5 THE EMPOWERED INVESTOR: A NEW PARADIGM OF INVESTING

1. Hass, Hans, 1970, *Energon: The Hidden Secret*, 18–30.
2. In a pivotal article in the *American Naturalist*, Dean Amadon highlights the importance of specialization. Using observations of the monotremes and primitive insectivores which are highly specialized for subterranean niches, Amadon argues that advances in evolution are the result of specialization. Similarly, George Simpson refers to the

king crab, which has flourished almost unchanged since the Triassic, and observes that, "Far from dooming it to extinction, its specializations seem almost to be a recipe for group immortality" (Simpson, 1941, p. 17). The authors report evidence to illustrate that major new species have evolved from highly specialized ones. A specialized group of fish, for example, learned to breathe air and walk on their fins, eventually giving rise to vertebrates. A specialized family of the Reptilia gave rise to birds and another to mammals. Birds of paradise, known for their high level of specialization, have allowed a high rate of mutation by natural selection (*Sources*: Amandon Dean, 1943, Specialization and Evolution, *The American Naturalist*, Vol. 77, No. 769, Simpson George, 1941, PALEONTOLOGY, The role of the individual in evolution, *Journal of the Washington Academy of Sciences*, Vol. 31, No. 1).

3. According to evolutionary biology, life forms constantly evolve and evolution selects the most "efficient" strategies for survival. For example, animals have acquired a foraging behavior akin to what physicists have calculated as the most efficient manner to find hidden objects; their search process is optimized, subject to specific constraints such as speed and eyesight, as well as distribution of prey (*Source*: Benichou, Coppey, Moreau, Suet and Voituriez, 2005, Optimal Search Strategies for Hidden Targets, *Physical Review Letters*, Vol. 94, No. 19).

4. Puempin, Cuno, and Wolfgang Amann, 2005, *Strategische Erfolgspositionen* (Verlag Paul Haupt Ber), 60–62.

5. Ancient Military, The Roman Military, online edition 2010, www.ancientmilitary.com/roman-military.htm

6. Apple Inc., 2010, Quarterly Report Pursuant of Apple Inc. Executive Summary, The Security Exchange Act: United States Securities and Exchange Commission, 19–21.

7. Morgan, John, and Herman Danelle, 2009, Apple Inc. Case study, *Strategic Management*, 10–14.

8. Stalk, George, Evans Philip, and Shulman Lowrence, 1992, Competing on Capabilities: The New Rules of Corporate Strategy, *Harvard Business Review*, March-April 1992.

9. Hamel, Gary, and Prahalad C.K., 1990, The Core Competences of the Corporation, *Harvard Business Review*, May–June.

10. MarketsData, 2012, markets.ft.com, Audi AG market data, *online Edition*, May 17, http://markets.ft.com/research/Markets/Tearsheets/Financials?s=NSUX:GER

11. Reiter, Chris, March 1, 2012, Audi Beats Mercedes, Targets Steady 2012 Profit, *Bloomberg, Online Edition*. http://www.bloomberg.com/

news/2012–03–01/audi-targets-steady-2012-earnings-after-beating-mercedes.html

12. The principle of building on strengths is also practiced in nature. The rabbit and the gazelle come to mind, both of which have evolved slim and powerful bodies to increase their running speed. Likewise, the Phasmida's camouflage and the Viceroy butterfly's mimicry of the toxic monarch are strengths developed through centuries of evolution. In all such cases, unique strengths developed by the evolutionary process drive survival.

13. Clausewitz, Carl V., 1909, *On War*, 200–202.

14. The efficient frontier is a set of assets (portfolio) that has the best possible expected return for a given risk level. (Elton, Edwin, and Gruber, Martin, 2011, *Investments and Portfolio Performance*, 382–383).

15. Buffett, Warren, 2009, To the Shareholders of Berkshire, *Shareholders report*.

16. Taleb, Nassim, 2011, *The Black Swan: The Impact of the Highly Improbable* (Random House).

17. See Appendix for short biographies of our interview partners.

18. Lauren, Kannry, December 23, 2008, Gallup.com, New Gallup Book Destroys the Myth of the Well-Rounded Leader, *Online Edition*. http://www.gallup.com/press/113536/press-release-strengths-based-leadership.aspx

19. Gladwell, Malcolm, 2001, *Outliers, The Story of Success* (Little Brown and Company), 49–52.

20. http://www.modelt.ca/background.html

21. Alizon, Fabrice, Shooter Steven, and Simpson Timothy, 2009, *Henry Ford and the Model T: Lessons for Product Platforming and Mass Customization*, 588–605.

22. Keynes, John Maynard, 1938, *Concentrated Investment Portfolios*, www.maynardkeynes.org/concentrated-stock-portfolios.html

23. Investopedia, Think like Warren Buffet, http://www.investopedia.com/articles/stocks/08/buffett-style.asp

24. Buffett, Mary, and Clark, David, 2006, *The Tao of Warren Buffett: Warren Buffett's Words of Wisdom*, 82–84.

25. Federer, Roger, 2010, during a presentation at the Hall of Fame in Switzerland.

26. Federal Reserve, Bank of New York, 2010, Operating Policy: Statement Regarding Purchases of Treasury Securities, *Online Edition*, November 3, http://www.newyorkfed.org/markets/opolicy/operating_policy_101103.html

27. Vanguard Precious Metals and Mining (ticker: VGPMX) is one of the funds to receive five-star ratings from Morningstar Ratings for funds. (Real Wealth, 2010, Silver Mutual Funds Offer an Option for Investors: The Simple Guide to Silver, *Silver Monthly*, 28–30.)

28. Seagreaves, Jim, 2011, Gold mutual funds, Alternatives to Gold, *Online Edition*, July 28, http://www.silvermonthly.com/gold-mutual-funds/

29. World Gold Council, 2011, Gold Demand Trends, Shareholders' Report, 21–23.

30. Canis, Bill, and Yacobucci, Brent, 2010, *The U.S. Motor Vehicle Industry: Confronting a New Dynamic in the Global Economy*, 3–5.

31. In a short sale, the investor borrows a stock from brokers and then sells it in the market, with the hope of earning a profit by buying the stock back again after the price falls. (For further elaboration see: Mishkin, Frederic S., and Eakins, Stanley, 2009, *Financial Markets and Institutions*, 141–143.)

32. Reyburn, Scott, 2012, Bugatti Collector Warns on Market, Owns World's Most Pricey Car, *Online Edition*, May 18, http://www.bloomberg.com/news/2012-02-21/bugatti-collector-warns-on-market-pays-more-than-30-million-for-top-car.html

33. Fraser, Paul, 2012, Chevrolet fans are in for a treat at Mecum Auctions' next classic cars sale so far, July 30, http://www.paulfrasercollectibles.com/News/CLASSIC-CARS/2011-News-Archive/Chevrolet-fans-are-in-for-a-treat-at-Mecum-Auctions'-next-classic-cars-sale/7226.page?catid=341

34. Rogers, Jim, June 2012, Rogers Holdings's Jim Rogers Predicts Recession, on media.bloomberg.com, http://search1.bloomberg.com/search?content_type=all&max_age=0&page=24&q=jim_rogers&sort=2

35. Johnson, G., Scholes, K., and Whittington, R., 2005, *Exploring Corporate Strategy: Exploring Techniques of Analysis and Evaluation in Strategic Management* (Pearson Education Limited), 7th edition, 113–115.

36. Pühringer Gruppe; ZZ1 Fund documentation. See also Festschrift 15 Jahre ZZ Vermögensverwaltung, Wien 2011, 52–54.

37. Aktienkurs, Phoenix Solar, 2012, Phoenix Solar AG share price in EUR, *Online Edition*, July 30. http://www.finanzen.ch/aktien/Phoenix_Solar-Aktie?rd=fn

38. McNeilly, Mark, 2001, *Sun Tzu and the Art of Modern Warfare*, 194–196.

39. Lewin, Ronald, 1998, *Montgomery As Military Commander*, 371–373.

40. For examples see Tjemkes, Brian, Vos Pepijn and Burgers Koen, 2012, *Strategic Alliance Management* (Routledge); for the importance of

networks in a special industry see Goedeking, Philipp, 2010, *Networks in Aviation: Strategies and Structures* (Springer).

41. Macdonald, Scott, and Gastmann Albert, 2004, *A History of Credit Power in the Western World*, 119–121.

42. History of Banking, The Fugger Dynasty: 15th–16th Century AD, October 2012, http://www.historyworld.net/wrldhis/PlainTextHistories.asp?groupid=2453&HistoryID=ac19&gtrack=pthc

43. Uzzi, Brian, and Dunlap Shannon, 2005, *How to Build Your Network*.

44. Granovetter, Mark, 1973, The Strength of Weak Ties, *The American Journal of Sociology*, Vol. 78, No. 6.

45. Porter, Michael,1996, *What Is Strategy?*

46. Grant, Robert, 2010, *Contemporary Strategy Analysis and Cases*, 244–246.

47. Templeton, Lauren, 2012, Our investment philosophy in practice can be summarized in one simple piece of investment wisdom, *Online Edition*, August 17, http://laurentempletoninvestments.com/

48. Kahneman, Daniel, and Tversky Amos, 2000, *Choices, Values, and Frames* (Cambridge University Press).

49. Antoine Henri de Jomini, Wikipedia, en.wikipedia.org/wiki/Antoine-Henri_Jomini

50. Hart, Liddel, 1941, *The Strategy of Indirect Approach*.

51. Related to the indirect approach is the element of surprise. In the military the indirect approach enables the strategist to surprise his enemy. The concept of the indirect approach has much deeper rules related to human behavior which can be found in other fields such as music and theatre.

52. Ineichen, Alexander, 2002, *Absolute Returns: The Risk and Opportunities of Hedge Fund Investing* (John Wiley and Sons).

53. Allen, Paul 2011, *Idea Man: A Memoir by the Co-founder of Microsoft*, Position 4309 Kindle e-book version.

54. Keynes, John Maynard, 2003, *The General Theory of Employment, Interest and Money*, (1st edition 1936). Harrod, R.F., 1990, *The Life of John Maynard Keynes*, http://www.maynardkeynes.org/keynes-the-speculator.html

55. Wikipedia, 2012, LTCM, October 16. http://en.wikipedia.org/wiki/LTCM

56. Wikipedia, 2012, Victor Niederhoffer, October 16, http://en.wikipedia.org/wiki/Victor_Niederhoffer

57. Wikipedia, 2012, Nicholas Maounis Amaranth, October 16, http://en.wikipedia.org/wiki/Amaranth_Advisors

58. Chua Amy, 2007, *Day of Empire: How Hyperpowers Rise to Global Dominance – and Why They Fall* (First Anchor Books Edition).
59. Taleb, Nassim, April 2011 *Nassim Taleb on Living with Black Swans*, Interview on Knowledge at Wharton, http://knowledge.wharton.upenn.edu/article/nassim-taleb-on-living-with-black-swans/
60. Biggadike, Ralph, 1979, *Corporate Diversification: Entry, Strategy, and Performance* (Harvard University Press).
61. Walsh, Carl, 2004, FRBSF Economic Letter Oct 1969, Federal Reserve Bank SanFrancisco, www.frbsf.org/economic-research/publications/economic-letter/2004/ december/october-6-1979
62. Yousuf, Hibah, 2011, Silver: $50 milestone coming 'any day now', *Online Edition,* April 25, http://money.cnn.com/2011/04/25/markets/silver_gold_prices_record/index.htm
63. A put option is a contract that gives the owner the right to sell a financial instrument at a specific time on a predetermined date. For more details see Mishkin, Frederic, and Eakins, Stanley, 2009, *Financial Markets and Institutions,* 656–658.
64. Artico, 2011, *Investment Objective and Investment Policy,* 10–12.
65. Allen, Paul, 2011, *Idea Man: A Memoir by the Co-founder of Microsoft*, Position 4309 Kindle e-book version.
66. Poston, Toby, 2006, The legacy of JK Galbraith, *BBC News,* http://newsvote.bbc.co.uk/mpapps/pagetools/print/news.bbc.co.uk/2/hi/business/4960280.stm
67. Iba, Hitoshi, and Aranh Claus, 2012, *Practical Applications of Evolutionary Computation to Financial Engineering: Robust Techniques for Forecasting, Trading and Hedging,* 84–86.
68. Hirsch, Jeffrey, and Perry Bill, 2012, *The Little Book of Stock Market Cycles, How to Take Advantage of Time Proven Patterns,* 5–7.
69. Erten, Bilge, and Ocampo José Antonio, 2012, *Super-Cycles of Commodity Prices since the Mid-nineteenth Century*, DESA Working Paper, No. 110, 6–8.
70. Lahart Justin, 2012, A Summer Rally Really Would Mean a Lot, *Online Edition,* April 29, xhttp://online.wsj.com/article/SB10001424052702304723304577370511539838288.html
71. Jansen, Jim, 2011, *Understanding Sponsored Search: Core Elements of Keyword Advertising,* 74–76.
72. Ferguson, Niall, 2009, *The Ascent of Money: A Financial History of the World,* (Thorndike Press).
73. Reinhart, Carmen, and Rogoff Kenneth, 2011, *This Time is Different: Eight Centuries of Financial Folly*, Princeton University Press.

74. Arnault, Bernard, 2005, TalkAsia Interview Transcript, March 16, http://articles.cnn.com/2005–03–16/world/talkasia.arnault.script_1_brands-creativity-business-growth/5?_s=PM:WORLD

75. Being impatient, especially when making decisions about short-term options, is an innate characteristic of human beings. Experiments by psychologists suggest that people tend to act more impatiently when making decisions about shorter-term options than longer-term ones; they do not discount future outcomes at a constant exponential rate. For further elaboration see for example Shane, Frederick, Loewenstein, George, and O'Donoghue, Ted, 2002, Time discounting and Time preference: A critical review, *Journal of Economic Literature*, Vol. 40, No. 2, 351–401; Laibson, David, 1997, Golden Eggs and Hyperbolic Discounting, *The Quarterly Journal of Economics*, Vol. 112, No. 22, 443–477; or Shefrin, Hersh, and Thaler, Richard, 1988, The Behavioral Life-Cycle Hypothesis, *Economic Inquiry*, Vol. 26, No. 4, 609–643.

76. Business Knowledge Center, 2012, Opportunity Cost, *Online Edition*, October 14, http://www.netmba.com/econ/micro/cost/opportunity/.

6   TWO PATHS TO YOUR INVESTMENT STRATEGY

1. Mintzberg, Henry, 1987, *Crafting Strategy*, Harvard Business Review, July–August.

2. Mintzberg, Henry, 1990, The Design School: Reconsidering the Basic Premises of Strategic Management, *Strategic Management Journal*, Wiley Online Library.

7   WHAT SHOULD AN EFFECTIVE INVESTMENT STRATEGY CONTAIN?

1. Bennis, Warren and Nanus Burt, 1985, *Leaders – The Strategies for Taking Charge*, Harper & Row, 87–89.

2. *Source*: Aeris Capital, family office of an SAP co-founder.

3. It is interesting to note that strategic investors sometimes have an entrepreneurial spirit which is reflected in their investment approach. In the case of Rolland-Yves, his focus investments were sometimes pure investments, but mostly investments with an entrepreneurial element of adding value by taking the molecule through clinical development, leveraging on the know-how and expertise of his privately held company.

4. Capital market theory applies a completely different approach. Here the asset allocation is defined by using the volatility measure according to the Gauss normal distribution. The possibility of power law events is not integrated and there is always the danger that the investor ends up with too little cash. This is why we propose an approach where financial needs in absolute figures (cash needs for maintaining the standard of living over three to five years) are used as a guideline for the security portfolio.
5. Historically gold has been an excellent hedge against inflation and has played a central role in the security portfolio. Given the volatility of gold prices over past few years, one may consider placing it in the diversification portfolio.
6. Markowitz, Harry M., 1991, *Portfolio Selection: Efficient Diversification of Investments,* Wiley, 2nd edition.

8   PUTTING THE PROCESS OF STRATEGIC INVESTING INTO PRACTICE

1. Randers, Jorgen, 2012, *2052: A Global Forecast for the Next Forty Years* (Chelsea Green Publishing).
2. Kahneman, Daniel, 2011, *Thinking, Fast and Slow,* p. 222 ff.

REFERENCES

Akerlof, George A., and Shiller, Robert G., 2009, *Animal Spirits: How Human Psychology Derives the Economy, and Why it Matters for Global Capitalism* (Princeton University Press), 130–134.

Aktienkurs, Phoenix Solar, 2012, finanzen.ch says Phoenix Solar AG share price in EUR, *Online Edition,* July 30.

Allen, Paul, 2011, *Idea Man: A Memoir by the Cofounder of Microsoft* (Porfolio), Position 4309 Kindle e-book version.

Alizon, Fabrice, Shooter Steven B., and Simpson Timothy W., 2009, *Henry Ford and the Model T: Lessons for Product Platforming and Mass Customization*, Elsevier, 588–605.

Alumni Association, 2005, Standford Research Institute, The SRI Alumni Newsletter: *History Corner*, 1–10.

Álvarez-Nogal, Carlos, and Chamley Cristophe, 2011, Debt Policy under Constraints between Philip II, the Cortes and Genoese Bankers, working paper, Universidad Carlos III de Madrid, 11.

Amadon, Dean, 1943, Specialization and Evolution, *The American Naturalist*, 77(769).

Ancient Military, 2010, Acientmilitary.com says The Military of Ancient Egypt, *Your Ancient Military Resource*, October 10.

Ancient Military, 2010, Acientmilitary.com says The Roman Military, *Your Ancient Military Resource*, October 10.

Apple Inc., 2010, Quarterly Report Pursuant of Apple Inc. Executive Summary, The Security Exchange Act: United States Securities and Exchange Commission.

Arnault, Bernard, 2005, articles.cnn.com says Chairman of LVMH, TalkAsia Interview Transcript, *CNN World*, March 16.

Artico, 2011, Investment Objective and Investment Policy, *Artico Dynamic Prospectus,* 10–12.

Battle of Salamis, 2012, britannica.com says the Battle of Salamis, *Encylopedia Britannica Online*, Retrieved October 15.

Bénichou, O., Coppey, M., Moreau, M., Suet, P. H., Voituriez, R., 2005, Laboratoire de Physique Théorique de la Matière Condensée (CNRS-UMR 7600), Université Paris 6, France, *Physical Review Letters [2005, 94(19):198101]*.

Bennis, Warren, and Nanus Burt, 1985, *Leaders – The Strategies for Taking Charge* (Harper & Row, New York), 87–89.

Biggadike, Ralph E., 1979, *Corporate Diversification: Entry, Strategy, and Performance* (Harvard Business School Press).

Board of Financial Stability, 2011, *Potential Financial Stability Issues Arising from Recent Trends in Exchange-Traded Funds* (ETFs), 1–4.

Brealey, Richard, and Myers Stewart, 2010, *Principles of Corporate Finance* (McGraw-Hill), 214.

Buffett, Mary, and Clark David, 2006, *The Tao of Warren Buffett: Warren Buffett's Words of Wisdom* (Scribner), 82–84.

Buffett, Warren E., 2009, To the Shareholders of Berkshire, *Shareholders Report*, Berkshire Hathway Inc.

Business Knowledge Center, 2012, netmaba.com says Opportunity Cost, *Economics Online Edition*, October 14.

Canis, Bill, and Yacobucci Brent D., 2010, The U.S. Motor Vehicle Industry: Confronting a New Dynamic in the Global Economy, *Congressional Research Service*, 3–5.

Chua, Amy, 2009, *Day of Empire: How Hyper powers Rise to Global Dominance – and Why They Fall* (Anchor, Reprint edition), 1–5.

Clausewitz, Carl V., 1909, *On War* (Project Gutenberg License 2006 EBooks edition,1946), 200–202.

Clausewitz, Carl V., 1942, *Principles of War* (The Military Service Publishing Company), 15–18.

Cuthbertson, Keith, Nitzsche Dirk, and O'Sullivan Niall, 2010, Mutual Fund Performance Measurement and Evidence. *Financial Markets, Institutions & Instruments*, 19, 2, 1, May 2010.

Davidsson, Markus, 2012, Large Impact Events and Finance, *Accounting and Finance Research*, Sciedu Press, 1, 1, 95–97.

Dimson, Elroy, Marsh Paul, Staunton Mike, McGinnie Paul, and Wilmot Jonathan, 2012, Credit Suisse Global Investment Return Source Book 2012, *Research Institute*, 37–59.

Elton, Edwin J., and Gruber, Martin J., 2011, *Investments and Portfolio Performance* (World Scientific), 382–383.

Erten, Bilge, and Ocamp José Antonio, 2012, *Super-cycles of Commodity Prices since the Mid-nineteenth Century*, working paper, UN-DESA and Colombia University, 6–8.

Farmer, J. Doyne, and Geanakoplos John, 2008, *Power Laws in Economics and Elsewhere*, 5–7.

Federal Reserve, Bank of New York, 2010, newyorkfed.org says Operating Policy: Statement Regarding purchases of Treasury Securities, *Online Edition*, November 3.

Ferguson, Niall, 2009, *The Ascent of Money: A Financial History of the World*, (Penguin Books), 127–132.

Fernandez, Pablo, and Del Campo Javier, 2010, *Return of Mutual Funds in Spain 1991–2009*, (IESE Business School).

Festschrift 15 Jahre ZZ Vermögensverwaltung, Wien 2011, 52–54.

Fraser, Paul, 2012, Paulfrasercollectibles,com says Chevrolet fans are in for a treat at Mecum Auctions' next classic cars sale so far, *Classic Car News Archive*, July 30.

Federer, Roger, 2010, the Jury Hall of Fame.

Gajek, Lestaw, and Ostaszewski Krzystof M., 2005, *Financial Risk Management for Pension Plans* (Elsevier), 333–335.

Gladwell, Malcolm, 2001, *Outliers, The story of Success* (Little Brown and Company), 49–52.

Goedeking, Philipp, 2010, *Networks in Aviation: Strategies and Structures* (Springer).

Granovetter, Mark, 1973, The Strength of Weak Ties, *American Journal of Sociology*, 78, 6, 1360–1380.

Grant, Robert M., 2010, *Contemporary Strategy Analysis and Cases* (Wiley, 7th edition), 244–246.

Groseclose, Elgin, 1934, *Man and Money: A Survey of Monetary Experience* (University of Oklahoma Press), 106–108.

Gross, Bill, 2012, *Investment Outlook: The Lending Lindy* (PIMCO).

Hall, William K., 1980, *Survival Strategies in a Hostile Environment* (Harvard Business Review), 75–85.

Hamel, Gary, and Prahald C.K., 1990, *The Core Competences of the Corporation* (Harvard Business Review), 13–15.

Harrod, R.F., 1990, *The Life of John Maynard Keynes* (Easton Press).

Hart, Liddel, 1941, *The Strategy of Indirect Approach* (Faber, London), 2–4.

Hass, Hans, 1970, *Energon: The Hidden Secret* (Molden), 18–30.

Hirsch, Jeffrey A., and Perry Bill, 2012, *The Little Book of Stock Market Cycles, How to Take Advantage of Time Proven Patterns* (Wiley), 5–7.

History of Banking, historyworld.net says The Fugger dynasty: 15th–16th century AD, October 2012.

Iba, Hitoshi, and Aranh Claus C., 2012, *Practical Applications of Evolutionary Computation to Financial Engineering: Robust Techniques for Forecasting, Trading and Hedging* (Springer), 84–86.

Ineichen, Alexander, 2002, *Absolute Returns: The Risk and Opportunities of Hedge Fund Investing* (Wiley, 1st edition).

Inverco, 2009, Asociación de instituciones de inversión colectiva y fondos de pensiones, *Memoria*, 9–10.

Investment Company Institute, 2012, *Investment Company Fact Book: A Review of Trends and Activity in the U.S. Investment Company Industry* (52nd edition), 18–20.

Investopedia, 2012, Nasdaq.com says Think like Warran Buffett, *Investopedia NASDAQ*, July 12.

Jansen, Jim, 2011, *Understanding Sponsored Search: Core Elements of Keyword Advertising*, (Cambridge University Press), 74–76.

Johnson, Gerry, Scholes Kevan, and Whittington Richard, 2005, *Exploring Corporate Strategy: Exploring Techniques of Analysis and Evaluation in Strategic Management* (Pearson Education Limited, 7th edition), 113–115.

Kahneman, Daniel, 2011, *Thinking, Fast and Slow* (Farrar, Straus and Giroux), 222–224.

Kahneman, Daniel, and Tversky Amos, 2000, *Choices, Values, and Frames* (Cambridge University Press).

Keynes, John M., 2003, *The General Theory of Employment, Interest and Money* (1st edition, 1936).

Keynes, John M., 1938, maynardkeynes.org says Concentrated Investment Portfolios, *Personal Webpage*, October 12.

Lahart Justin, 2012, online.wsj.com says A Summer Rally Really Would Mean a Lot, *Wall Street Journal, Online Edition,* April 29.

Laibson, David, 1997, Golden Eggs and Hyperbolic Discounting, *The Quarterly Journal of Economics,* 112, 22, 443–477.

Lauren, Kannry, 2008, Gallup.com says New Gallup Book Destroys the Myth of the Well-Rounded Leader: Strengths Based Leadership Explains Why People Follow Leaders, *Online Edition,* July 20.

Lewin, Ronald, 1998, *Montgomery As Military Commander* (Da Capo Press), 371–373.

Liddell Hart, Basil Henry, 1943, *Thoughts on War* (Faber & Faber, London).

Lubove, Seth, 2010, Washingtonpost.com says Classic Cars can Cost Millions, But are They Good Investments? *The Washington Post, Online Edition*, July 30.

Macdonald, Scott B., and Gastmann Albert L., 2004, *A History of Credit Power in the Western World* (Transactions publishers), 119–121.

Mandlebrot, Benoit, and Hudson, Richard L., 2008, *The (Mis)Behavior of Markets, Profile Books* (Profile Books), 523–536.

MarketsData, 2012, markets.ft.com says Audi AG market data, *Thomson Reuters, Online Edition,* July 20.

Markowitz, Harry M., 1991, *Portfolio Selection: Efficient Diversification of Investments* (Wiley, 2nd edition)

Mauldin, John, and Tepper Jonathan, 2011, *Endgame: The End of the Debt Supercycle and How It Changes Everything* (John Wiley & Sons, Inc.), 86–87, 206–207.

McNeilly, Mark R., 2001, *Sun Tzu and the Art of Modern Warfare* (Oxford University Press), 194–196.

Michael, Porter, 1997, *How Competitive Forces Shape Strategy* (Harvard Business Review).

Mintzberg, Henry, 1987, *Crafting Strategy* (Harvard Business Review).

Mintzberg, Henry, 1990, The Design School: Reconsidering the Basic Premises of Strategic Management, *Strategic Management Journal* (Wiley Online Library).

Mishkin, Frederic S., and Eakins, Stanley G., 2009, *Financial Markets and Institutions* (Pearson International Edition), 127–658.

Morgan, John, Herman Danelle, 2009, Apple Inc. Case Study, *Strategic Management,* 10–14.

Noble, Thomas, Strauss Barry, Osheim Duane, Neuschel Kristen, and Accompo Elinor, 2007, *Western Civilization: Beyond Boundaries* (Wadsworth Publishing).

Porter, Michael E.,1996, What Is Strategy? *Harvard Business Review*, 10–12.

Porter, Micheal, 1997, How Competitive Forces Shape Strategy.

Poston, Toby, 2006, newsvote.bbc.co.uk says The Legacy of JK Galbraith, *BBC News.*

Puempin, Cuno, 1981, *The Practice of Strategic Management* (Swiss Volsbank), 25–26.

Puempin, Cuno, 1993, *How World Class Companies became World Class* (Gower Publishing Company).

Puempin, Cuno, 1987, *The Essence of Corporate Strategy* (Gower Business Enterprise Series).

Puempin, Cuno and Pedergnana, Maurice, 2008, *Strategisches Investment Mangement* (Haupt Verlag AG), 24–26.

Randers, Jorgen, 2012, *2052: A Global Forecast for the Next Forty Years* (Chelsea Green Publishing).

Real Wealth, 2010, Silver Mutual Funds Offer an Option for Investors: The Simple Guide to Silver, *Silver Monthly*, 28–30.

Reinhart, Carmen M., and Rogoff Kenneth S., 2011, *This Time is Different: Eight Centuries of Financial Folly* (Princeton University Press).

Reiter, Chris, 2012, Bloomberg.com says Audi Beats Mercedes, Targets Steady 2012 Profit *Bloomberg, Online Edition*, July 30.

Reyburn, Scott, 2012, Bloomberg.com says Bugatti Collector Warns on Market, Owns World's Most Pricey Car, *Online Edition*, May 18.

Rogers, Jim, 2011, youtube.com says Missing out on Commodities [Video], *Investbox*, October 12.

Rogers, Jim, 2012, bloomberg.com says an interview on the Economy, September 2012.

Ross, Stephan A., Westerfield Randolph W., and Jaffe Jeffrey, 2010, *Corporate Finance* (Mcgraw-Hill College), 247–249.

Rowling, Sheryl L., 2008, *Tax and Wealth Strategies for Family Businesses* (CCH Inc.), 212–214.

Seagreaves, J.D., 2011, Silvermonthly.com says Gold mutual funds, Alternatives to Gold, *Silvermonthly, Online Edition*, July 28.

Shane, Frederick, Loewenstein George, and O'Donoghue Ted, 2002, Time Discounting and Time Preference: A Critical Review, *Journal of Economic Literature*, 40, 2, 351–401.

Shefrin, Hersh M, and Thaler, Richard H., 1988, The Behavioral Life-Cycle Hypothesis, *Economic Inquiry*, 26, 4, 609–643.

Sim, Jack, 2011, *Britsh Defence Doctrine*, Joint Doctrine Publication.

Simpson, George, 1994, Paleontology: The Role of the Individual in Evolution, *Journal of Washington Academy of Sciences*, 31, 1–20.

Stalk, George, Evans Philip, and Shulman Lowarence E., 1992, *Competing on Capabilities: The New Rules of Corporate Strategy* (Harvard Business Review).

Taleb, Nassim N., 2010, *The Black Swan: The Impact of the Highly Improbable* (Random House Trade Paper, New York), xxi–xxii, 209–211.

Templeton, Lauren, 2012, laurentempletoninvestments.com says Our Investment Philosophy in Practice can be Summarized in One Simple Piece of Investment Wisdom, *Online Edition*, August 17.

The Prize in Economics, 1990, Nobelprize.org says The Prize in Economics-Press Release, July 23.

Thornburg Investment Management, 2013, *A Study of Real Real Returns, Strategies for Building Real Wealth*, 19, 1–4.

Tjemkes, Brian, Vos Pepijn, and Burgers Koen, 2012, *Strategic Alliance Management*, (Routledge).

Tzu, Sun, 1910, *The Art of War: The Oldest Military Treatise in the War* (Oriental Printed Books and Manuscripts, British Museum), 71–157.

Tzu, Sun, 2011, scienceofstrategy.org says Sun Tzu's life, *The Science of Sun Tzu*, Aug 1.

Uzzi, Brian, and Dunlap Shannon, 2005, How to Build Your Network, *Harvard Business Review*, 3–5.

Welch, Jack, 2012, brainyquote.com says Vision Quotes, November 4.

Wikipedia, 2012, Wikipedia.org says Nicholas Maounis Amaranth, *The Free Ecncylopedia, Wikimedia Foundation, Inc.*, October 16.

Wikipedia, 2012, Wikipedia.org says LTCM, *The Free Ecncylopedia, Wikimedia Foundation, Inc.*, October 16.

Wikipedia, 2012, Wikipedia.org says The Battle of Salamis, *The Free Ecncylopedia, Wikimedia Foundation Inc.*, May 17.

Wikipedia, 2012, Wikipedia.org says Victor Niederhoffer, *The Free Ecncylopedia, Wikimedia Foundation Inc.*, October 16.

Williamson, David, Cookie Peter, Jenkins Wyn, and Moreton Keith Michael, 2004, *Strategic Management and Business Analysis* (Butterworth-Heinemann), 85–86.

World Gold Council, 2011, Gold Demand Trends, Shareholders' report. Full year 2011.

Yahoo finance, 2012, finance.yahoo.com says the historical prices for S&P-500 (^GSPC), September 15.

Yousuf, Hibah, 2011, money.cnn.com says Silver: $50 milestone coming "any day now", *CNN Money, Online Edition*, April 25.

Zhanghong, Ru, and Zhang Xiao, 1970, *Chinese Characters History Lessons*, 1, 1–3.

Printed and bound by CPI Group (UK) Ltd, Croydon, CR0 4YY